the
Weekend
Crafter®

Feltmaking

the
Weekend
Crafter®

Feltmaking

Fabulous Wearables, Jewelry & Home Accents

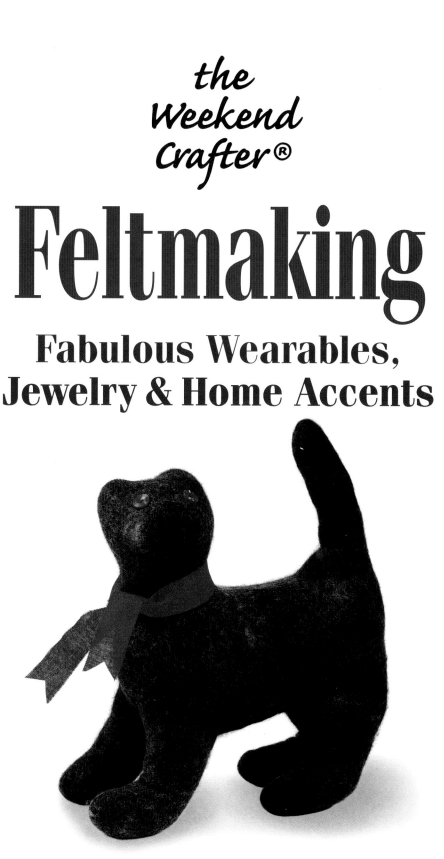

CHAD ALICE HAGEN

LARK BOOKS

A Division of Sterling Publishing Co., Inc.

NEW YORK

EDITOR:
MARTHE LE VAN

ART DIRECTOR:
SUSAN MCBRIDE

PHOTOGRAPHY:
EVAN BRACKEN

COVER DESIGNER:
BARBARA ZARETSKY

ILLUSTRATIONS:
ORRIN LUNDGREN

ASSISTANT EDITOR:
VERONIKA ALICE GUNTER

SPECIAL PHOTOGRAPHY:
BETH BEEDE

10 9 8 7 6 5 4 3 2 1

First Edition

Published by Lark Books, a division of
Sterling Publishing Co., Inc.
387 Park Avenue South, New York, N.Y. 10016

© 2002, Chad Alice Hagen

Distributed in Canada by Sterling Publishing,
c/o Canadian Manda Group, One Atlantic Ave., Suite 105
Toronto, Ontario, Canada M6K 3E7

Distributed in the U.K. by Guild of Master Craftsman Publications Ltd., Castle Place,
166 High Street, Lewes, East Sussex, England
BN7 1XU
Tel: (+ 44) 1273 477374, Fax: (+ 44) 1273 478606, Email: pubs@thegmcgroup.com,
Web: www.gmcpublications.com

Distributed in Australia by Capricorn Link (Australia) Pty Ltd.,
P.O. Box 704, Windsor, NSW 2756 Australia

A Note About Suppliers
Usually, the supplies you need for making the projects in Lark books can be found at
your local craft supply store, discount mart, home improvement center, or retail
shop relevant to the topic of the book. Occasionally, however, you may need to buy
materials or tools from specialty suppliers. In order to provide you with the most
up-to-date information, we have created a listing of suppliers on our Web site, which
we update on a regular basis. Visit us at www.larkbooks.com, click on "Craft Supply
Sources," and then click on the relevant topic. You will find numerous companies
listed with their web address and/or mailing address and phone number.

If you have questions or comments about this book, please contact:
Lark Books
67 Broadway
Asheville, NC 28801
(828) 253-0467

Printed in China

ISBN 1-57990-252-9

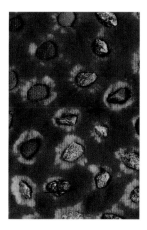

CONTENTS

Introduction..6

A Short History of Felt 7

Materials 9

Tools 16

Techniques 18

Spiraling Bracelet 32

Wandering Path Chair Pad...............................34

"Roll, Snake, Roll!" 36

The Perfect Little Bag 38

The Amazing Felted Door Stop 40

Twist Bracelets 42

Pocket Bears 44

Here, Kitty, Kitty 46

Miracle Bead Necklace 48

Marvelous Mittens 51

Coffee Cozy..54

Fuzzy Pumpkin Throw.......................................57

Journal Cover 60

Sweet Snuggle Slippers 63

Hugs and Kisses Beret......................................66

Double Puzzle Table Runner 69

Airy Fairy Scarf...72

Hand-Quilted Pillow..74

Acknowledgments...77

About the Author 77

Templates 78

Index...80

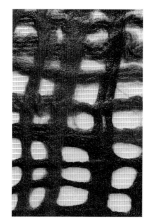

INTRODUCTION

Welcome to the ancient craft of making felt from wool. If you haven't tried to make felt before, you're in for a delightful, magical time. If you're an advanced felter, or a beginner wanting to learn more, each of these projects will add to your skills.

Feltmaking is about simplicity and discovery. All you need is wool, water, soap, and some form of agitation, such as rubbing with your hands, to produce a solid and unique piece of fabric. As you continue to explore feltmaking, you'll discover that differing breeds and ages of sheep produce different types of wool. The temperature of the water, variety of soap, and how the wet wool is rubbed—all can change the shape, thickness, and density of the felt. As you can see by these variables, a whole world of possibilities awaits you, the patient explorer.

Felting materials and techniques have come to us through more than 2,600 years of feltmaking. Today, we're making felt almost in the same fashion that it has been made since before the 6th century B.C. There is something enchanting about this long tradition of feltmaking. We feel as if we are never truly alone—we're in partnership with the sheep, the shepherds, the current generation of feltmakers around the world, and the feltmakers throughout all of history.

I designed the projects in this book to acquaint you with a variety of different ways to make felt. I hope

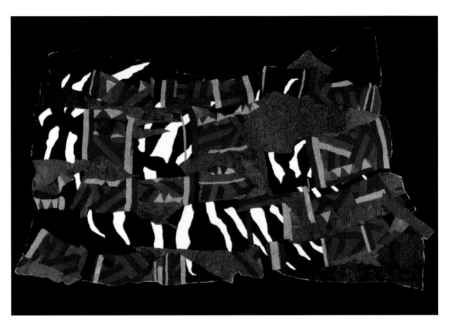

Chad Alice Hagen. *Histories R Felt Undercasement, 1989*. 53 x 81 inches (134.6 x 205.7 cm). Hand-felted wool. Photo by Gerald Sedgewick.

you'll enjoy creating these projects and eventually will develop your own. There are really no right or wrong ways to make felt; it's simply that some felts will turn out more successful than others. Every project, each new fleece, even a different soap teaches you something new. Amazingly, every felter felts a different way, forming her own special method to create her particular type of felt. This will also happen to you as long as you maintain an awareness of what the wool is doing beneath your hands and remain persistent in your exploration.

I discovered the world of handmade felt in 1979, and I became a full time feltmaker and artist in 1982.

My time is divided between teaching feltmaking, producing a line of felt wearables, and creating large felt artworks for corporate and private collections.

Why do I felt? I absolutely love how wool absorbs and holds color. Wool can whisper faint hints of tonalities or be totally drenched and dripping with color. I love the smell and feel of wool, wet or dry, and how easily an idea can take a solid, felted shape. I teach extensively to show students the ease and flexibility of handmade felt, and how learning to make felt enriches one's artistic life. I hope you, like me and countless others around the world, become intrigued with hand-felted wool.

A SHORT HISTORY OF FELT

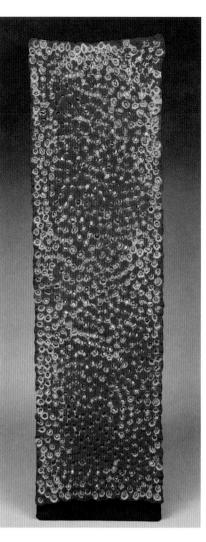

Chad Alice Hagen. *Driveway Collection 3, 2000*. 54 x 16 inches (137.2 x 40.6 cm). Hand-felted wool, wrapped limestone, mica. Photo by Tim Barnwell.

When asked if they know anything about felt, most people remember the felt craft squares they used in elementary school. However, handmade and commercially made felt can be found all around us. Wool felt's unique properties of sound and thermal insulation, absorption, and resiliency have lent themselves to thousands of uses in the modern and ancient world, such as clothing, furnishing, decorative items, and even homes.

What is felt? Felt is made from sheep wool. The wool, a renewable resource, is clipped off the sheep. If you take a small handful of the wool, soak it in soapy water, and roll it between your hands, in a few minutes you may have a felted ball. It can be that simple. But as you learn about wools from different sheep and experiment with various felting methods, you'll discover how versatile felted wool is to work with. You can make flat felt, cut

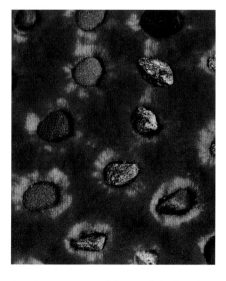

Chad Alice Hagen. *Driveway Collection 3, detail*. Photo by Tim Barnwell.

Mongolian women "quilting" a design through thick layers of a felt rug. Photo by Beth Beede.

Mongolian woman pulling, rolling, and felting wool to make boots. Photo by Beth Beede.

it up, and sew it into clothing and artwork. If you place a sheet of plastic between layers of wool, you can make seamless bags, hats, or boots. Thick, huge sheets of felt can be placed over a stick framework and made into an extremely comfortable winter home. The possibilities of felt are endless.

Because it doesn't require complicated tools or machinery, hand-felted wool probably predates weaving and spinning. There are tall tales about Noah discovering wool felt on the floor of the ark. Most likely, however, early sheep and goat herders developed the ability to make felt after observing the matting of fleece on sheep skins when worn on their bodies as clothing.

Some of the oldest felt remnants found have been dated to Neolithic people (6500–6300 B.C.) in Turkey. Early Bronze Age (2000–800 B.C.) felt caps have been found in Denmark and Germany. The most exciting examples of a highly evolved feltmaking technology date from the 7th to the 2nd century B.C. Pieces of felt were preserved in frozen burial tombs in the Altai Mountains in Siberia. Many of those examples can be seen in the Hermitage Museum in St. Petersburg, Russia. In 1979, some of these felted items were exhibited at the British Museum, inspiring many to try their hand at this ancient art.

Nomadic sheep-herding peoples continue their feltmaking traditions to this day. Hand-felted coats and rugs, among other items, were not only a necessity in cold, windy climates, but were also developed into economic livelihoods. Beautiful felted rugs still can be found in many Middle Eastern and Central Asian markets. In the cold Scandinavian north countries, nothing was better than hand-felted clothing and boots for protection from cold winters and snowy seas. Hand-felted baby clothing and diapers are still being made and worn. Distinctive hand-felted hats were developed over time to identify various ethnic groups throughout Eastern Europe and Asia.

Contemporary textile artists in Europe and America have been exploring feltmaking since the late 1960s. Feltmaking as a historic textile process was included in most textile history classes. A few feltmaking pioneers such as Carole Beadle, Joan Livingstone, and Barbara Setsu Pickett were experimenting in the early 1970s.

In 1975 the exhibit *From the Lands of the Scythians—Ancient Treasure from the Museums of the USSR* traveled through North America. Included with the striking examples of Scythian gold work were many pieces of the Hermitage Museum's ancient felt from the Pazirik Tombs. This exhibit brought feltmaking to the attention

of many people, inspiring textile artists to start exploring the historic technique, creating a modern revival of the feltmaking art.

As enthusiasm for feltmaking grew, important books were written on the subject, and more exhibitions of contemporary and traditional feltmaking were mounted. By 1994, numerous contemporary felt exhibitions had been held in the United States and in Europe, bringing the work of international feltmakers to a greater number of viewers and artists. International conferences on feltmaking flourished and continue today as a vital forum where information and techniques are exchanged. Participating textile artists return home to share their knowledge and increase interest in feltmaking.

Feltmakers have enlisted modern technology for their ancient craft by organizing and publishing informational newsletters. Feltmakers also have an Internet e-mail listserv where both beginning and professional feltmakers can ask questions, share ideas, and form regional meetings. The ancient feltmaking tradition continues to flourish today, thanks to the dedicated teaching of accomplished feltmakers and their passionate desire to share their craft.

MATERIALS

As a feltmaker, you won't be investing a lot of money in tools and materials. All you need to create felt are three basic supplies: wool, soap, and water.

Wool

Freshly sheared wool is coated with oils and sheep sweat, and may contain bits of dirt, straw, and grass. Commercial wool processors first wash the wool to remove the oil (converting it to lanolin), and then treat the wool to remove most of the straw and grasses. The wool is next run through a carding machine that has several rollers covered with short wires. The machine combs the wool fibers so they all lie parallel to each other. The wool is then removed from the carder in either a thick rope called a *sliver* or a *roving*, or in wide, thin sheets that are stacked on top of each other and called a wool *batt*.

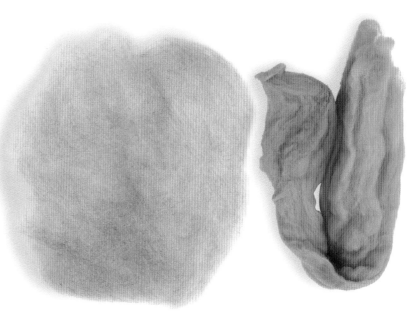

Wool batt (left) and wool sliver (right)

It's important to choose the right wool for your projects. Although other ingredients are essential—soap helps the wool felt because it can lower the pH of the wool; hot water makes the wool fiber contract and stretch; and hard agitation can help make a dense felt—choosing the right wool is at the heart of a successful felt project.

How does one start finding the right wool to felt? It's useful to understand why wool felts, and how the scales, crimp, and thickness of the fibers give each fleece its unique character. Knowing this can help you decide what wool is best for a particular project.

THE SCALES

Each wool fiber is covered with overlapping *scales*. This is the particular quality of wool that gives it the ability to felt. The scales are attached only at their lower end, and the top of the scales point toward the tip of the wool fiber as shown in figure 1. When water is absorbed into the wool, the fibers swell up, causing the scales to open outward much like an open pinecone. When the wet wool is pressed or rubbed, the pressure on the open scales causes the fiber to move toward

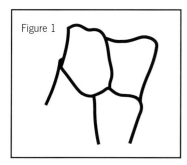

Figure 1

its root end. Repeated pressure and rubbing moves the fibers closer and closer together, forming a densely entangled mass. The felt appears to shrink, but the fiber actually is becoming more tangled.

THE CRIMP

Crimp refers to the curl of the wool fiber. The size and amount of crimp is determined by the breed and sometimes the age of the sheep. The wool crimp is created by two types of cells in the cortex of the wool fiber—the ortho-cortex cells and the para-cortex cells (see figure 2). These two cell types are arranged in different shapes and amounts depending on the sheep breed. The ortho-cortex cells are found on the outside of the crimp curl and easily absorb water. The para-cortex cells, found on the inside of the curl, don't absorb as much water. When the wool fiber is soaked with soap and water, the ortho-cortex cells absorb more moisture and swell, extending lengthwise in a corkscrew shape. This lengthening and contracting of the cortex cells help the wool fiber to move, entangle, and felt.

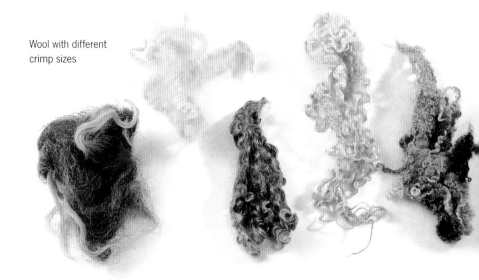

Wool with different crimp sizes

THICKNESS OF THE FIBER

The thickness of the wool fiber also determines how well it will felt and for what projects it is best suited. Long wool fibers with thick diameters are less flexible, but these longer fibers are able to entangle with more fibers and produce a strong, stiff felt. This type of wool can be excellent for durable projects such as rugs and chair cushions. Fine wool fibers have thin diameters and can be packed densely together when felted. Fine wool fibers make smooth, lightweight, and drapable felt.

The amount of crimp, size of scale, and thickness of the wool fiber are all related. Very curly wool has more crimp in the fiber which means the scales are smaller, and the wool is finer, giving a matte appearance. Coarse, thicker fibers have larger, loose curls. These fibers are covered with large flat scales which reflect a great deal of light, giving a glossy sheen.

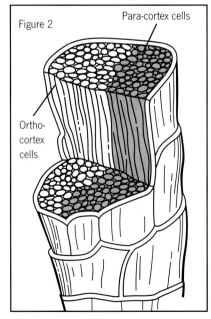

Figure 2

Para-cortex cells

Ortho-cortex cells

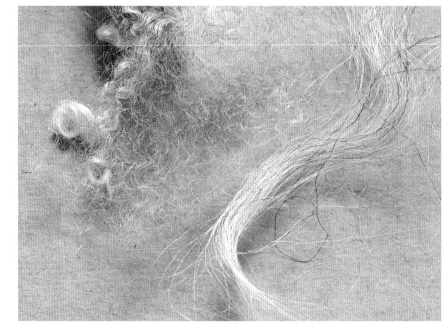

Wool with different fiber thicknesses

CHOOSING THE RIGHT WOOL FOR THE PROJECT

The focus of this book is to provide an introduction to feltmaking through interesting felted projects that can be completed in a weekend or less. Merino or Pelssau/Gotland wools are recommended for each of the projects, so you won't have to sample the shrinkage and felting ability of different wools. I chose these two wools based on their distinctive qualities, and, most importantly, their ease of felting. However, once your interest is captured by the magic of felting, you may want to experiment with other wools.

Merino wool comes primarily from Australia, although there are many American Merino growers as well. Merino is the finest wool you can find. People who experience contact dermatitis as a result of wearing wool can usually wear Merino wool. Merino is perfect for most wearables, such as scarves, hats, mittens, and slippers. Merino doesn't work very well for objects that will be subjected to heavy use, such as a rug. Merino is also very useful for decorative parts of projects such as prefelt. Merino shrinks about 45 percent during the felting process.

Scandinavian Pelssau/Gotland wool is very fast felting. I'm using a 50 percent Pelssau/Gotland and a 50 Norwegian long wool blend. Pelssau/Gotland wool blend comes in a rectangular batt composed of carded wool layers. This is a wonderful wool for projects that need strength and durability, such as chair cushions and rugs. I also like to use it for stuffed animals, doorstops, and paperweights. Pelssau/Gotland wool shrinks about 40 percent while being felted.

Merino
wool slivers

Olive oil soap bars

Soap

You'll need to make three soap mixtures prior to starting a feltmaking project. The *basic soap gel* is a gelatinous soap and water mixture. It's the most concentrated formula from which the other two mixtures are made. The basic soap gel is never directly applied to the wool during feltmaking. The *soap gel mix* is made from water mixed with the basic soap gel. It has a fairly thick and slimy consistency. Use the soap gel mix as a lubricant on your hands as you felt the wool. *Wetting Mix* is the soap gel mix further diluted with water. You'll use the wetting mix to moisten the wool.

Soap works in several ways to help felt wool fibers. One way is by changing the wool's pH—the measurement of its acidity or alkalinity. On a scale of 0 to 14, a pH measure of 7 indicates neutrality. This number increases with alkalinity and decreases with acidity. Wool is normally 4.9 pH. When saturated in a soap-and-water mixture between 9 and 11 pH, wool fibers will swell, pushing out their scales, causing faster felting. Above 12 pH, wool loses its elasticity and breaks down.

Soap also serves as a lubricating medium, helping the wool fibers to move around each other. At the soft felt stage, soap helps your hands glide over the felt's surface without disturbing any fibers. Later, at the hard felt stage, soap prevents the pilling of the felted surface as you rub. Too much soap, however, retards the felting process by keeping the fibers from entangling with each other.

While just about any soap or dish-washing detergent will do, I prefer to use a gel made from French olive oil soap. This particular soap has a 9–10 pH, thereby helping the wool felt faster. French olive oil soap is very economical. A 16-ounce (453.6 g) block will make 1 gallon (3.8 L) of basic soap gel, which is further diluted into a soap gel mix and a wetting mixture. Olive oil soap is kind to your hands; it doesn't dry your skin like other soaps and detergents. Additionally, olive oil soap isn't overly sudsy, and it rinses out very fast. Greek olive oil soap doesn't create a gel like the French olive oil soap, but you may want to experiment with this variety. There are other soap options, such as laundry flakes dissolved in water, bar soap, goat's milk soap, and many more. Each soap has its devotees, and each soap will take some getting used to. Directions for mixing the solutions will vary if you use an alternate soap.

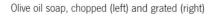

Olive oil soap, chopped (left) and grated (right)

MAKING THE BASIC SOAP GEL

The basic soap gel does take a day to prepare, so plan accordingly.

Grind or grate the block of olive oil soap in a food processor or with a hand grater. Place the grated pieces in a sturdy 1-gallon (3.8 L) plastic container or bucket. (Olive oil soap is very slippery. For safety reasons, always use plastic containers instead of glass.) Bring 14 cups (3.3 L) of water to a boil, and add it to the grated soap. Vigorously stir the soap and water with a strong wire wisk. Cover the container, and let it sit for a day until the entire mixture solidifies.

French olive oil soap is also sold in smaller 8-ounce (226.8 g) bars. To make the basic gel with this amount of soap, mix 3½ cups (.83 L) of boiling water with the grated soap.

Grinding the soap in a food processor

Gelatinous soap gel

MAKING THE SOAP GEL MIX

Add 1 cup (237 ml) of the basic soap gel to 3 cups (.71 L) of warm water in a 1 quart (1 L) container, and stir well with a wire whisk. You can use this soap gel mix immediately. It will feel very slimy between your fingers, but you'll learn to love and appreciate its texture. The soap gel mix thickens as it sits, but this is no problem. This soap gel mix provides lubrication during the soft and hard felting stages.

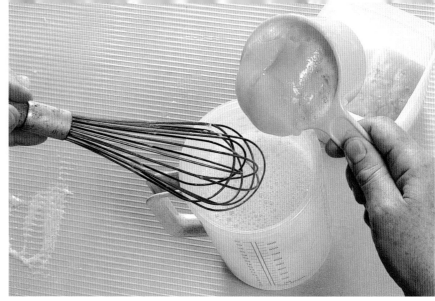
Making the soap gel mix

MAKING THE WETTING MIX

In a 1 gallon (3.8 L) sturdy plastic bucket, add 1 cup (237 ml) of the soap gel mix to 12 cups (2.8 L) of warm water. Use the wire whisk to very thoroughly blend the mixture. It should feel slippery when rubbed between your fingers. Use this wetting mix to wet the dry wool prior to soft felting.

TIPS ON WHEN TO USE EACH SOAP MIXTURE

If the fibers start sticking to your hands, add more wetting mix to the felt surface. If the surface is rough, starts to pill, or needs more lubrication, add more soap gel to your hands. There is probably too much soap on the felt if its surface starts feeling sticky. You should add a little more wetting mix until the surface feels more lubricated.

Soap gel mix has a thick consistency

Making the wetting mix

Soap containers

ORGANIZING YOUR SOAP CONTAINERS

While felting, you'll need to have several containers of the different soap mixtures on your work table. In the photo above you'll see (clockwise from top): a 1-gallon (3.8 L) container of the basic soap gel; a 1-gallon (3.8 L) container of the wetting mix ; a 1-quart (1 L) container of the soap gel mix; a 1-pint (473 ml) container of the same soap gel mix (the smaller container is easier to use during the felting process); a small ½-cup (118 ml) dipper-style container for added control when you pour the wetting mix onto the dry wool; and a 1-gallon (3.8 L) tub as a rinse bucket for wringing wet sponges and catching drips when squeezing the felt project.

RINSING OUT THE SOAP

Take as much care removing the soap from the felt as you did applying it. Remember that hot water is a felting tool, and it should be used accordingly. If your felt project is close to the desired size, use cool water and gentle squeezing to rinse out the soap. If your felt project needs to shrink a bit more or become more dense, use hot water and vigorously rub the felt to remove the soap. Check each project's directions for specific water temperatures.

VINEGAR RINSE

Always follow the cool or hot water rinse with a vinegar rinse to return the wool to pH 4.9 and help close the wool's scales. Fill a large 1-gallon (3.8 L) bucket with cool water. Add about 2 tablespoons (29.6 ml) of white vinegar. Rinse the felt in this solution, and squeeze dry.

WATER

Water is essential to making hand-felted wool. Water is absorbed into the wool fibers, causing them to swell. Swelling causes the overlapping scales (the cuticle) on the outside of the fiber to lift. Water also causes the crimp, or curl, of the wool fiber to lengthen and contract. Both of these actions help the wool fibers move and connect with each other.

The temperature of the water is also an important felting tool. Wool felts more quickly if the water temperature is between 104° and 122°F (40° and 50°C). However, using water that hot is not always comfortable for your hands. Also, using very hot water too early in the felting process may cause just the surface of the wool to felt, leaving the interior wool fibers loose and unfelted. Water that is too hot, over 140°F (60°C), changes the elasticity of the crimp so that the wool fibers may not return to their original size.

For the projects in this book, we will use lukewarm water mixtures to wet the wool fibers and to felt. For our purposes, lukewarm water will be defined as a temperature that is comfortable to your hand. We will use hot water (as hot as your hands can stand) as a felting tool for rinsing some projects. Vigorous rubbing and rinsing with hot water further shrinks and tightens the wool fibers and creates a denser felt.

Hard water that has a high amount of minerals like calcium or iron may cause problems. Hard water can react with your felting soap and form curds or indissoluble matter that is hard to rinse out. If you live in a hard water region and don't have a water softener connected to your home water supply, try putting your felting water in a 5-gallon (18.9 L) container and adding 1 teaspoon (4.9 ml) of water softener. Water softener is sold in most grocery stores.

Always monitor the amount of water in your felt. Too much water can prevent the wool fibers from coming in contact with each other and felting. Wool fibers will absorb as much water as they can, up to 12 times their weight. The excess water will puddle around your felt project. If this puddle of water starts moving toward the edge of your work surface, use a household sponge or towel to absorb it.

TOOLS

For the projects in this book, you'll use several tools to help with the felting process.

Your **hands** always will be the most useful tools. Your sense of touch will tell you what stage the felt is in before your eyes can even tell a difference. For this reason, try not to wear gloves while felting. If the soap irritates your skin, experiment with a different soap. Take off all your rings, and store them in a safe place, as any protruding stones and settings can rip the soft felt.

The best felting mat combination consists of a **clear plastic**, **ridged shelf liner** with a **nonskid mat** underneath. Both items are sold as shelf and drawer liners. The clear plastic ridged mat is usually packaged in 10-foot (3 m) rolls of several widths. This felting mat combination is placed flat on your work surface, and the wool is rubbed against it in different ways to help the fibers entangle and felt. The small ridges on the shelf liner give just the right amount of friction for both gentle

Clockwise from top: food scale, ridged plastic lid with handle, towel, sushi mat, sponges

Clear plastic, ridged shelf liner over a non-skid mat

and hard felting and help to contain water. For most of the projects in this book, a 24 x 24-inch (61 x 61 cm) felting mat combination is fine. You'll need a longer felting mat, approximately 8 to 10 feet (2.4 to 3 m) long, for projects such as the Fuzzy Pumpkin Throw on page 57 and the Airy Fairy Scarf on page 72.

Towels and **ordinary kitchen sponges** are necessary to mop up excess water. You also may want to wear an apron to protect your clothes from water and soap.

Plastic sheeting is useful for covering your entire work table to protect it from water and soap. You can use it to cut out resist patterns for some of the projects, too. Heavy (4 mil) plastic is easiest to use.

For some projects you'll need **cotton fabric** as a guide for laying out the wool. Use an inexpensive, lightweight cotton or cotton blend fabric.

A **permanent black marker with a medium point** is very useful for drawing forms and labeling plastic and fabric patterns. (Always label your patterns so you can remember what they are.) Make sure you test the marker to make sure it's waterproof.

High quality, sharp, pointed **sewing scissors** are very helpful for cutting out patterns and for cutting and trimming the felt as needed. Manicure scissors are great for cutting intricate patterns, such as those on the Double Puzzle Table Runner, page 69.

A **tape measure** will come in handy when you're measuring objects to determine the size of resist patterns and in countless other situations.

A small, inexpensive **postage or food scale** will help you to weigh the amounts of wool needed for projects.

A **small bamboo reed mat** (used for sushi making and found in most Asian food stores) is a good tool for quickly making snakes, dreadlocks, cording, and other long felted objects. Don't worry if you can't locate a bam-

Above, clockwise from top: plastic sheeting, scissors, black permanent marker, tape measure, ruler, calculator, sketchbook

Below, clockwise from top: straight pins, soft leather, wire pet brush, bias binding, needle, thread

boo reed mat; directions for using just your hands are also given.

Other useful tools include: **notebooks** for writing down hints that you discover and measurements needed for later projects; a **calculator** is great for figuring out shrinkage percentages; and an assortment of **plastic containers** and **mixing tools** (see Organizing Your Soap Containers on page 15). Some projects require specific tools for their completion. These will be discussed when they come into use.

Clever felters have devised countless other tools by altering the traditional uses of many everyday items, such as electric sanders, plastic container lids, bubble wrap, and so forth, to help them work efficiently. While it's fun to search out different objects to use in felting, the tools I've listed will be sufficient to create the projects in this book.

A Word about Safety

Wool is soft and friendly, but use common sense and be careful when felting. Soap and water mixtures are slippery and should be quickly mopped up if they drip on the floor. Always use plastic buckets and containers for water and soap mixes so you don't drop slippery containers. Be aware that some sinks have very hot water, and check before rinsing so you don't scald your hands. Clean up after felting. Hang all towels, sponges, and especially sushi mats up to dry or they will begin to smell and mold. Hand lotion is great to keep your hands smooth.

If you plan to do a lot of felting, consider getting a thick, heavy-duty floor mat to stand on to relieve leg discomfort. Keep your posture straight, and try to avoid bending your hands at the wrist. Raise your table to a good working height, about 2 inches (5 cm) below your bent elbow.

Basic Feltmaking Kit

To save time, I put my frequently used felting tools and materials in a bucket or box. This is my felting kit. Each project in this book uses all these supplies. When a project's supply list calls for the "basic feltmaking kit," this is what you should have in your bucket or box.

24 x 24-inch (61 x 61 cm) plastic, ridged felting mat*
Plastic nonskid mat
1-gallon (3.8 L) bucket of wetting mix
1-quart (1 L) container of soap gel mix
1-pint (.5 L) container of soap gel mix
1-gallon (3.8 L) rinsing bucket
Wetting mix dipper
Vinegar rinse
Towels
Sponges
Tape measure
Scissors
Black waterproof marker

*This size is fine for most projects. If you need a larger mat, it will be mentioned in the specific project's materials list.

TECHNIQUES

Felt balls and snakes are used in several of the projects in this book.

This section also covers the basic process for flat and resist felting.

Agitation

Agitation of the wet and soapy wool fibers is any controlled rubbing, rolling, or throwing of the felt with your hands or other felting tools. Agitation causes the wool fibers to move and entangle with each other, creating the felted fabric.

You'll use different agitation actions and tools at various times in the felting process and with different felted forms. Sometimes you'll barely touch the surface of the wet and soapy wool as you begin to felt, and at other times you'll toss the wet felt down on the table as hard as you can. The amount and force of any agitation depends on how dense or interlocked the wool fibers have become. A delicate scarf requires less agitation than a heavy chair cushion. In all types of agitation, the felt will shrink faster in the direction that you're rubbing or rolling. Knowing this allows you to adjust the size and shape of the felt you're creating. The main idea is to agitate the fibers until they interlock sufficiently for the project.

Basic Solid Felt Balls

Hand-felted balls are easy to make, and they are an ideal hands-on introduction to feltmaking. In this book, solid felt balls are used to make a fun and sophisticated bracelet (see the Spiraling Bracelet on page 32), but felt balls also can be used for buttons, pins, decorative embellishments on hats and clothing, pin cushions, cat toys, or simply placed in a bowl as a colorful design accent for any room.

WHAT YOU NEED

Basic feltmaking kit

Merino wool sliver

Note: We're using a single wool color for this basic project. As you continue to make felt balls, try experimenting with different colors for both the inside and outside of the ball.

1 Tear off several finger-length bits of wool, and place them in front of you on your work table. Take an additional fist-size amount of wool, and bunch it into a tight ball shape.

2 Dip the ball into the wetting mix, and thoroughly saturate it by squeezing it several times. Squeeze out about half of the wetting mix. Continue to shape the ball by squeezing and poking it with your fingertips for about one minute.

4 As soon as the wool ball is soapy and its fibers are holding together, roll the ball between the palms of your hands. Roll very gently and slowly at first. Increase the pressure of the roll only when the ball feels sturdy. With continued rolling, the ball will decrease in size as its wool fibers become more densely felted.

5 When the felt ball feels very hard and it is the size you want, rinse out the soap under hot water. Give the ball a few squeezes in a vinegar rinse. Squeeze out as much liquid as you can, re-roll the ball back into shape, and let it dry.

3 With dry fingers, pick up a piece of the finger-length wool, and tightly wrap it around the wet felt ball. Dip the ball into the soap gel mix. Repeat this step, wrapping and dipping the ball, until it's about 50 percent larger than the final desired size.

Basic Solid Felted Snakes

Hand-felted "snakes" are actually long, flexible felted ropes that are very easy to make. Snakes can be used as straps (see The Perfect Little Bag on page 38), ties, and closures (see the Journal Cover on page 60), or just a friendly batch of brightly colored companions.

WHAT YOU NEED

Basic feltmaking kit

Merino wool sliver

Sushi mat

BEFORE YOU BEGIN

Determine the approximate thickness of your snake by taking the wool sliver and tightly twisting it between your fingers. For thinner snakes, divide the sliver lengthwise, twist-testing it until you find the thickness you want. The length of the snake is determined by the length of the wool sliver. If you want to make your snake longer, overlay the ends of the sliver, making sure that the overlaid area is as thick as the rest of the wool.

1 Divide a 12-inch-long (30.5 cm) wool sliver in half lengthwise. Use one of these halves as your test snake. Fold the sliver in your hand, and dip it into the wetting mix as shown. Squeeze the wool several times to saturate the fibers. Gently squeeze out excess wetting mix, unfold the sliver, and lay it down on the felting mat.

2 With outstretched fingers, lightly roll the sliver back and forth on your felting mat until the wool takes on a rounded shape.

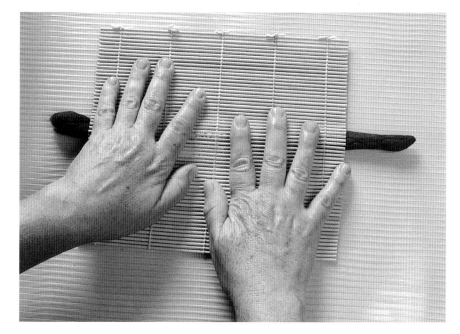

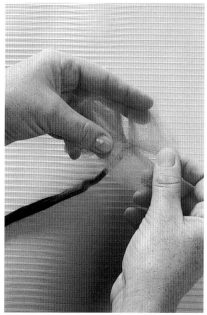

3 Place the sushi mat over the round soft snake. Very gently roll the mat and the snake back and forth until you feel the snake become firmer under the mat. Then, roll faster and harder until the snake is stiff enough to balance on your index finger like a pencil.

If you don't have a sushi mat, you can use your hands. With your fingers spread wide, roll the snake back and forth, moving your fingers from the center of the snake to the ends and back again. Roll gently at first until the snake gets firm, and then apply more pressure and speed until the snake is fully felted.

4 Rinse the snake under hot water, squeeze it several times in a vinegar rinse, and hang or lay flat on a towel to dry.

BASIC FELT DREADLOCK

You can make snakes with one dry end and then attach them to hats and berets (see the Hugs and Kisses Beret on page 66) or just about any other felted object. This snake variation, which I call a *dreadlock*, is added to the project just before starting the soft felting.

1 Figure the thickness of your dreadlock as you would for a snake (see Before You Begin, page 20). Consult the specific project directions to determine the dreadlock's length. Leave 3 inches (7.6 cm) of wool dry on one end of the sliver. This dry end is called the *root*. Protect the dry root end as you dip the sliver into the wetting mix as shown and proceed to felt the dreadlock following the instructions for Basic Felt Snakes.

2 Before attaching the felted dreadlock to your project, use your dry hands to open up the root end. Spread the ends of the dry fibers into an open circle, as you would when planting a tree. Pull the dry fibers hard against the felted dreadlock to make a secure root. Continue with the project as directed.

Note: Loops can be formed by making the dreadlock with two dry root ends (see the instructions for making basic felt dreadlock on this page).

Basic Flat Felt

Learning to make thin, very even, flat felt is a valuable skill. You'll avoid having bumps and thin spots in your slippers and other wearable projects. Smooth and even felt looks better and lasts longer. It's important to only work with small amounts of wool at a time. If you try to rush a project by laying out long, thick lengths of wool, you'll create uneven felt. It takes practice and patience to learn to divide small sections of fine Merino wool and properly lay it out, so be prepared to take your time and enjoy the process.

WHAT YOU NEED
Basic feltmaking kit
Merino wool sliver

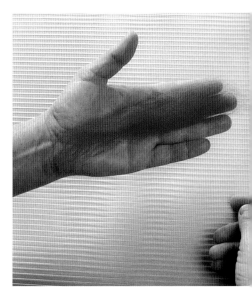

2 Take each thin length of wool sliver, and pull it apart in lengths as long as your hand. This is the amount of wool that you'll work with to lay out the wool layers.

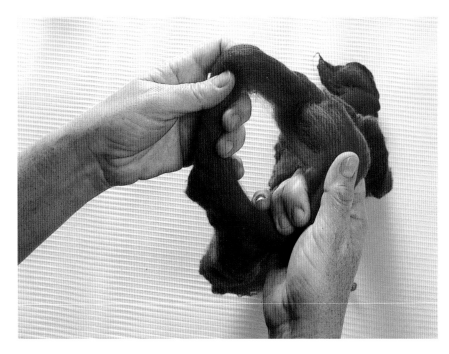

1 Tear off about 12 inches (30.5 cm) of wool sliver. Merino wool fiber is very long, so place your hands about 5 to 6 inches (12.7 to 15.2 cm) apart before gently pulling and separating. Also make sure the sliver isn't twisted (even a single twist makes it almost impossible to tear apart the wool). Estimating the center, use your thumbs and forefingers to divide the 12-inch (30.5 cm) sliver in half width-wise. Divide the two halves again, creating four thin lengths of wool sliver.

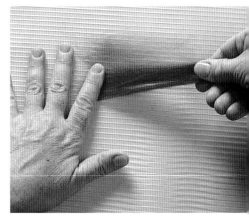

3 Hold the small length of sliver in your right hand pinched between your thumb and the side of your forefinger. Lay the other end of the sliver on the felting mat, and place the side of your left forefinger flat over the very end of the silver. Hold this finger down as you pull back with the right hand as shown. A very thin, even *shingle* of wool will pull out. Very gently pat this shingle down against the felting mat before moving on.

4 Using the process described in step 3, continue to lay out small thin shingles of wool across the felting mat. Place all the shingles side by side, making sure they're all going in the same horizontal direction. Overlap the thin tops and bottoms of the shingles (like shingles on a roof) until you've covered the area required for your project. Always pat down each new shingle to help condense its fibers before moving on. Look to see if there are any holes or thin areas in your wool layer. You may go back and lay down additional shingles to make a layer that is visually even. This first layer of wool should be so thin that you could read a newspaper through it. If there are thicker shingles in your layer, don't pick them out; just try to work more evenly next time. This is your first wool layer.

6 Lay down a third and then a fourth wool layer. Place each layer directly on top of the previous one, but facing the opposite direction. Remember to pat down the shingles. Once you've completed four layers, you've formed a *wool batt.*

7 Gently tuck in the wispy bits of wool that stick out beyond the edge of the wool batt. Don't fold the fibers under; just tuck them in.

5 Following the technique described in step 4, lay down a second layer of wool shingles. Work directly over the first layer but in the opposite direction so the fibers run top to bottom.

8 Place one hand flat on the wool batt. Use the dipping cup to sprinkle the wetting mixture over your hand as shown. Press down for a few moments until the wool absorbs the water.

9 Move your hand, and add more wetting mixture until the entire wool batt is saturated. The wool should appear to be flat and sticking to the felting mat with no air bubbles.

This is also the point at which you should add prepared prefelt designs or dreadlocks (see specific project directions).

10 Now you'll begin the soft felting process. Rub your palms with the soap gel mix as shown, and press straight down with your whole hand on the wet felt. Press down over the entire wool surface, adding more soap gel mix to your hands if the fibers are sticking to them. Alternate the pressing with a very gentle circular rubbing using your whole hand. Your hands should be moving on a layer of soap rather than directly on the wool. Continue pressing and rubbing until the felt feels sturdier, almost like a piece of fabric. At this stage, you should be able to run your fingertips across the felted surface without moving any fibers.

Tip: When you press your hand down on the newly wetted wool, soap and water should come up between your fingers. If it doesn't, add more wetting mixture. There will be a small puddle of soapy water oozing out about 1 to 2 inches (2.5 to 5 cm) around the edges of your project. Keep sponges scattered around your work surface to soak up any water in excess of that amount. As you continue felting and the fabric becomes denser, you'll notice that more water is released. Just soak it up with a sponge and squeeze it out in your rinse tub.

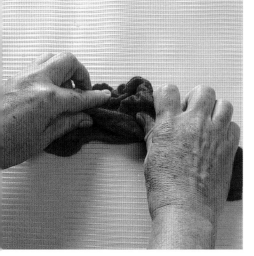

11 Pick up the felt, and slowly squeeze about three quarters of the soapy water into the rinse bucket. Continue to gently squeeze the felt, dipping it into the rinse bucket to wet it with soapy water between squeezes. You also may place the felt back on the mat as shown and gently knead and refold the felt, adding more soapy water until it feels firmer.

13 Test the felt by pinching the same spot top and bottom. If the felt fabric doesn't pull apart, proceed to the next step. If the pinch test fails, continue rubbing the felt between your hands and squeezing it.

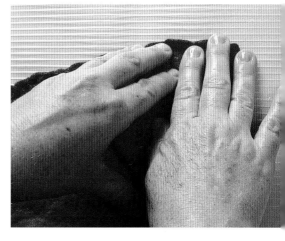

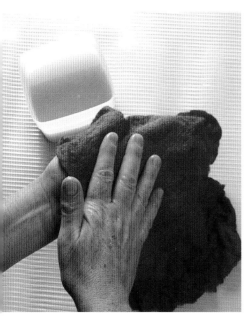

12 Pick up the felt, and gently rub it between your hands with plenty of soap gel mix. (The warmth from your hands helps speed the felting process.) Be sure to rub the entire felt surface, especially the edges.

14 *Fulling* is the next process. The felt is now sturdy enough for you to apply harder agitation. Throwing the wet felt down onto a low table or clean sink as shown is a very useful way to further shrink the felt. (To throw the felt with the greatest effectiveness, make sure to bend your knees and raise both hands over your head.) Have enough soapy water in the felt so that it makes a loud thump when thrown. Add more wetting mix now and then if the felt seems dry. You should be able to tell a big differ-ence in the density and size of the felt after it's thrown. Follow specific project directions for the number of throws.

15 Lay out the felt on the mat, and measure it with the tape measure. If you need to felt some more, firmly rub the felt across the ridges on the mat with your hands. Rub hard, keeping enough soapy water in the felt to prevent pilling. If the edges of the felt are wavy, you may "spot felt" by rubbing specific areas that need shrinking as shown. Remember that the felt shrinks fastest in the direction it's rubbed.

16 When the felt is slightly larger than the final measurements, but is firm and well felted to the touch, rinse the soap out under a running tap. Use cool water and a gentle squeeze if the felt size is just about perfect. Use warm to hot water and rough squeezing if the felt could be more dense or smaller in size.

17 Dip the felt in a vinegar bath, squeeze, and lay flat on a clean surface. You may steam iron the felt to make it flatter if directed to do so in the project instructions. Hang the felt over a drying rack or clothes hanger to dry. Place towels underneath the felt to catch dripping water.

Basic Prefelt Designs

Adding hard-edged shapes and design motifs to a felted object is fairly easy. The Marvelous Mittens on page 51 and the Double Puzzle Table Runner on page 69 use prefelted wool to create stunning patterns. Prefelt is simply flat, lightly felted wool. It's made like basic flat felt, but prefelt is only felted to step 13, the point where small shapes won't fall apart when cut out. If prefelt is felted too long, its fibers felt to each other and will not entangle with the loose fibers on your project.

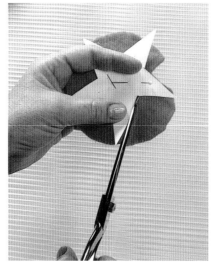

Photo 1

Photo 2

Prefelt doesn't need to be rinsed after it's made because it will be rinsed once it's part of a felted project. Prefelt designs are cut out with scissors (photo 1) and placed on a wet project just before you start rubbing and felting the surface (photo 2). Prefelt designs can be added wet or dry. Once you place them on your project, add some soap gel mix to your hands, and then lightly rub the prefelt with your flat hand for about two to three minutes. Once the prefelt adheres, don't attempt to pick it up and place it elsewhere. Continue felting your project, following the directions.

Basic Resist Felting

One of the advantages of working with hand-felted wool is that you can create three-dimensional objects without any noticeable seams. A plastic pattern, or *resist*, actually stays inside the wool layers while the project is being felted, keeping (resisting) the two sides from felting together. This process makes it possible to make smooth-fitting slippers and mittens, one-piece hats, and strong bags of any size. To lay out the wool for resist projects, you'll use the same skills you've learned for flat felting.

WHAT YOU NEED
Basic feltmaking kit
Merino wool sliver or Pelssau/Gotland batt
Plastic resist pattern, 5 x 8 inches (12.7 x 20.3 cm)*

*Each project that uses resist felting will give you specific directions for making the plastic pattern. The instructions on this page are for a felted bag.

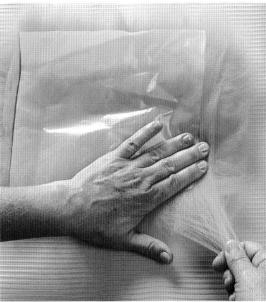

2 Pat down the wool batt with your hands, and then flip over the whole batt and pattern. Check to see if the wool extends evenly beyond the pattern edges. Carefully pull off any excess wool as shown, and add it to seams that appear thin. Remove the resist pattern, and place the layered wool batt in a safe place. This is the first side of your project.

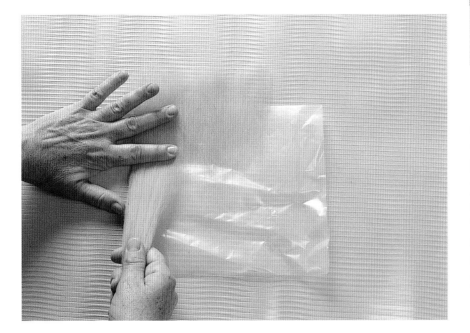

1 With the plastic resist pattern on the felting mat, divide the wool into two piles: one pile for one side of the plastic resist pattern, and the second pile for the opposite side. Divide each pile into four smaller piles, one for each individual layer. Cover the plastic pattern with these four thin layers of wool, each layer perpendicular to the last. The edges of the wool should extend about 1 to 1½ inches (2.5 to 3.8 cm) beyond the edges of the pattern in the direction you're laying down the shingles. These are your *seam allowances*.

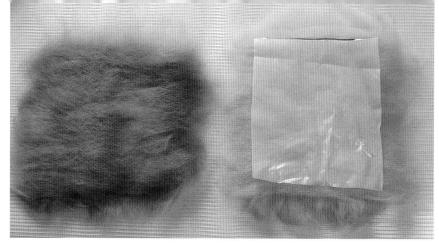

3 Repeat steps 1 and 2 to create the second side of your project. Flip over the wool batt, and leave it on the felting mat. Remove the plastic pattern.

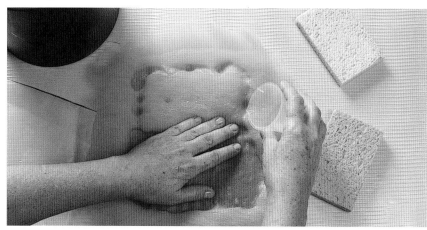

4 Use the dipper cup to gently pour a thin dribble of wetting mix about 1½ inches (3.8 cm) inside the edges of the wool batt as shown. Keep the wool dry outside of this water line. (The dry wool is your seam wool.) Soak the wool on the inside of the water line with the wetting mix. Press down on the wet wool with your hands, adding more wetting mix until the wool absorbs the water and appears to stick down flat to the felting mat.

5 Replace the resist pattern. If any wool underneath the pattern is dry, press and smooth your hands across the pattern to distribute water to the edges.

6 If your project has an opening (as when making a felt bag), pull back the plastic from the appropriate dry wool edge. Fold the dry wool over up to the water line as shown. Replace the plastic over the dry wool, and press down to wet.

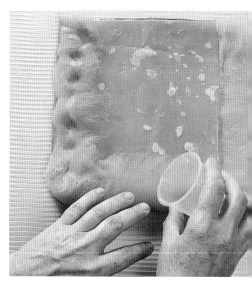

7 Fold the dry seam edges over the pattern. Make sure you fold the wool very close to the edge of the pattern without actually folding the plastic. Dribble a **tiny** amount of wetting mix over the dry wool to help it stay in place (see photo).

8 Take the other dry wool batt, and place it exactly on top of the wet wool batt, matching the edges carefully on all four sides.

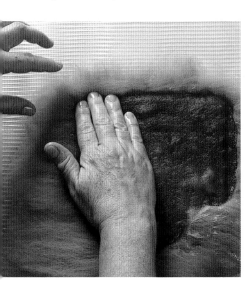

9 Using the dipper and your hands, soak the center of the dry batt with the wetting mix until you feel the edge of the plastic pattern under the wool. Keep the wool dry beyond the edge of the pattern.

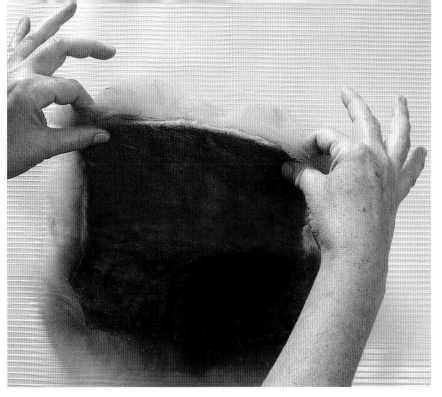

10 Using the thumbs and index fingers of both hands, pick up all three layers (the bottom wool, the pattern, and the top wool) at the top corners of the project, and flip over. Lift the project high so the dry wool seam edges don't fold under.

11 If you're making an opening in your project, finish it now by bending back the wet wool and the pattern at the opening's edge. Fold in the dry seam wool to the water line as shown. Replace the top pattern and wet wool, pressing the opening edge to wet the bottom layer of wool. Don't worry if the pattern slightly sticks out beyond the wet wool.

12 Fold over the rest of the dry seam wool on the wet center wool as shown. Press the wool down, and add more wetting mix if needed.

This is also the point at which you should add prepared prefelt designs or dreadlocks (see specific project directions).

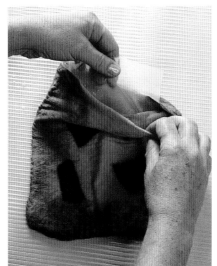

13 Rub some soap gel mix on your hands, and press them firmly down on the wool surface. Water and suds should come up between your fingers. Continue to press down over the entire surface, forcing out air bubbles and compressing the fibers. With more soap gel mix on your hands, start lightly rubbing the wool surface very gently like you would rub a butterfly's wing. Move your hands in a circular direction inward from the edges. (If you circle outward, you may push the seam off the project surface.) Keep a layer of soap between your hands and the surface of the wool. Make sure no wool fibers are moving under your hands. If fibers start to stick to your hands or the surface loses lubrication, add more soap gel to your hands. Continue to alternate pressing and gently rubbing until the surface feels firmer, and you can drag your finger across it without moving any fibers. This may take 10 to 20 minutes depending on the size of the project. Flip the felt over, and gently press and rub the second side until it feels as firm as the first side.

14 Following specific project instructions, remove the pattern, and start felting the project from both the inside and outside.

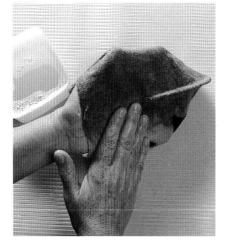

15 Place one hand inside the felt, and hold it flat against the seam area. Gently press open the ridge that may have formed at the edge of the pattern area.

16 If the ridge is large, try gently stretching it open with your fingers. Press or gently stretch all the ridges this way until they disappear. (If you rub the ridges without stretching them open, you might felt them into a permanent bump.)

17 With one hand on the inside, rub the felt between your open hands, moving twice around the entire project. Make sure to cover all areas and the edge. Add lots of soap gel mix so that you don't abrade the felt surface with your hands.

18 Gently squeeze the felt over a rinse tub about 15 times, turning the felt around in your hands and dipping it into the rinse water several times to keep it wet and soapy. Perform the pinch test to see how much the wool has felted. Pinch the felt fibers at the same spot on both sides of the fabric. The wool fibers should not gap apart. If they do, repeat step 17.

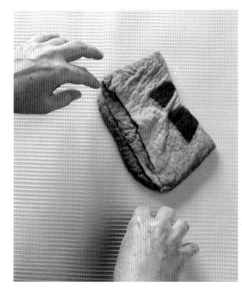

19 The felt is now strong enough to be thrown against a low tabletop or into a clean sink. Raise the wet felt over your head, and toss it down as hard as you can onto the table or sink. Do this as many times as directed in your project instructions. Follow the project directions for finishing the felt to the correct size, and rinsing. If no specific instructions are given, felt the project to the right size, and then rinse it out under cool water with gentle squeezing. If you want the project to shrink a bit more, use hot water and vigorous rubbing. Squeeze felt in a vinegar rinse and hang to dry.

Spiraling Bracelet

Expect a large number of admirers when you wear this striking and colorful felt bead bracelet. It's so soft and light you'll almost forget it's wrapped around your arm. No one needs to know just how simple it was to create.

WHAT YOU NEED

Basic feltmaking kit

½ ounce (14.2 g) red Merino wool sliver

1 ounce (28.4 g) black Merino wool sliver

2 additional 6-inch (15.2 cm) lengths of red and black Merino wool slivers

White craft glue

Wrist-size memory wire

Sharp hat pin or small-shafted awl

24 bone beads, white buttons, or light-colored beads

Pliers

Wire cutters

Strong quick-setting glue

2 end-cap beads

1 Following the Basic Solid Felt Ball instructions on page 18, divide the red Merino wool sliver into six equal portions to make six red beads. Divide the black Merino wool sliver into two piles. Divide one pile into 12 portions to make 12 small black beads. Divide the second pile into six portions to make six black beads. Gently roll the wet wool beads in your hands just long enough to make them fairly smooth. The beads should remain very squishy and wet.

2 With dry hands, pull off six thin 6-inch-long (15.2 cm) strips of both the red and the black slivers. Slightly roll each one between your hands to condense the wool fibers. Starting at the top, wrap one red sliver strip in a spiral pattern around and down a large black bead as shown. Holding both ends of the red stripe, dip the bead into the soap gel mix. Pat the spiral with your fingertips for about a minute; then gently roll the bead between your hands, taking care that the stripe stays adhered. Continue to roll the bead until it's hard and firm. Repeat this step for all six of the large black beads and all six of the large red beads. (Wrap the red beads with the black sliver.) Roll the 12 small black beads until they're hard and firm.

5 Straighten about 2 inches (5 cm) of one end of the memory wire. (This lets the wire easily follow the hole made by the hat pin or awl.) Using the sharp hat pin or small-shafted awl, carefully make a hole through the felt beads just before stringing (see photo).

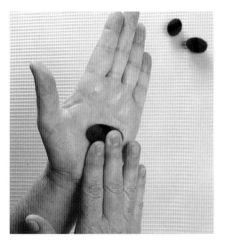

3 Vigorously rinse all the felt beads in hot water to remove the soap. Dry the beads by squeezing them in a towel. Give the larger wrapped beads an oval shape by rolling them very hard on the table or in your hands in only one direction (see photo). Let the beads completely dry.

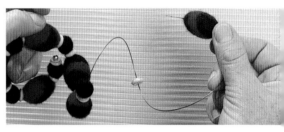

6 String the felt beads with the coordinating beads or buttons in the order shown. Trim the memory wire to 1 inch (2.5 cm) on each end of the strung beads.

4 Make a mixture of equal parts of the white craft glue and warm water. Place all the felt beads in the mixture and squeeze them several times, making sure they are saturated. Squeeze out most of the excess liquid. Roll the spiral beads back into their oval shapes. Let dry. The glue mixture hardens the beads and prevents them from getting too fuzzy.

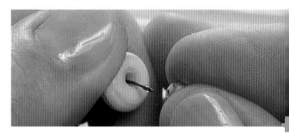

7 Place a small drop of the strong quick-setting glue on one end of the memory wire. Cover the wire with the end-cap bead. When the glue is dry, push all the beads toward the secured end. Trim the wire ¼ inch (6 mm) from the last bead. Place a drop of the glue on the wire, and cover it with the second end-cap bead.

Wandering Path Chair Pad

This wonderful and practical flat felted pad gives a soft touch to a hard chair. Warm, thick, and inviting, these one-of-a-kind household accents will provide you and your guests with a more comfortable dining experience. If you increase the project's size, you also can create a beautiful felted rug.

WHAT YOU NEED

Basic feltmaking kit

3½ ounces (99.2 g) light gray Pelssau/Gotland wool blend batt

½ ounce (14.2 g) dark gray Pelssau/Gotland wool blend batt

Knobbed plastic food container lid with a ridged underside, optional

Black double-fold extra-wide bias tape

Sewing machine

Straight pins

Needle and black sewing thread

Note: Karakul is a great substitute for the Pelssau/Gotland wool blend, especially if you decide to make a rug.

1 Separate the light gray Pelssau/Gotland wool batt into four thin layers as shown. Lay them into a 20 x 20-inch (50.8 x 50.8 cm) square. Place each layer down with its fibers perpendicular to the previous layer. Fold under any wool fibers that stick outside of the square, and then pat the edges straight. Place the wool batt on the felting mat, and saturate the wool with the wetting mix (see Basic Flat Felt, steps 8 and 9, on page 24).

2 Divide the dark gray wool batt into long ½-inch-wide (1.3 cm) strips. Lay them out on the felting mat, overlapping their ends. With damp hands, slightly roll the wool to consolidate its fibers.

4 Flip over the pad, and continue felting the back in the same manner (alternate pressing down the wool with gentle spiral rubbing). Rub any uneven spots along the edges to shrink them (see photo). Continue felting both sides of the cushion until you can drag your fingers across the surface without disturbing any fibers. At this stage, you can throw the pad about 50 to 100 times. Make sure the pad is very sturdy. It should be hard to fold in half.

3 Take the dark gray wool strip, and lay out a wandering line design as shown. Dip your hands into the soap gel mix, and very gently wet and rub the design for about five minutes until it attaches to the background. Start to felt the pad by pressing straight down on the wool with your hands. Alternate pressing with a very light rubbing of the entire surface in a circular motion. Continue these two actions for about 10 minutes, or until the wool surface begins to feel more solid when you run your fingers across it.

5 Rinse and vigorous rub the pad under hot water. Iron flat, and hang to dry.

6 Pin and machine-stitch the bias tape to the right side of the dry pad. Make the chair ties by folding a 40-inch (101.6 cm) length of bias tape and stitching it down the center. Cut the tape into two sections, and hem the ends. Machine-stitch the center of each tie along the bottom edge of the sewn binding at the rear corners of the pad. Flip the pad over, and finish by hand-stitching the bias tape to the back.

"Roll, Snake, Roll!"

This is a fun project for young children. You can capture their attention by acting out the little story of "Roll, Snake, Roll" (shown in bold). Make a whole vase full of colorful snakes, or tie them around your arms and ankles.

WHAT YOU NEED

Basic feltmaking kit

White Merino wool sliver, about 12 inches (30.5 cm) long

Red and yellow Merino wool slivers, small amounts of each

Sushi mat

1 **"Here's the backbone of the snake."** Make the snake's backbone by dividing the white Merino wool sliver in half. Lay the backbone on the felt mat.

2 **"Let's give the snake some clothes."** Alternate thin strips of the red and yellow Merino wool slivers in a 4 x 12-inch (10.2 x 30.5 cm) rectangle below the snake's backbone. Use the length of the snake's backbone to determine the length of the snake's "clothes." Lay the snake along the top edge of the "clothes."

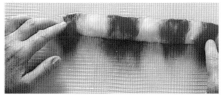

3 **"Let's give the snake a drink."** Dribble a small amount of wetting mix down the length of the snake's backbone. **"Let's roll the clothes on the snake, and give her another drink of water."** Roll the snake in the clothes like a jelly roll as shown. Dribble more wetting mix down the length of the clothed snake. **"Watch out, snake, a bicycle is coming."** Flatten the snake with your hands to completely saturate the wool.

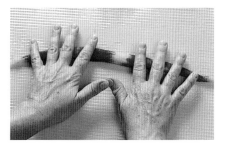

4 **"Ahh, we'll help fix the snake."** Use your fingers and thumb to pinch the wet wool back into a snake shape. Spread your fingers wide, and with your hands gently roll the snake back and forth on top of the felt mat five times, saying each time, **"Roll, snake, roll!"**

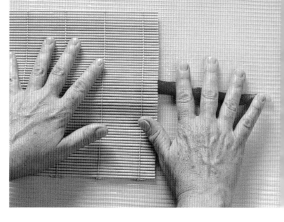

5 Place the sushi mat over half of the snake. Roll over the wool with one hand on the sushi mat and the other on the snake as shown. Roll five times, and then move the sushi mat to cover the opposite end of the snake. Roll another five times, continuing to chant, **"Roll, snake, roll."** As the snake gets stiffer, roll harder and faster with the sushi mat, causing the tail of the snake to flip back and forth. **"It's coming alive!"** Continue to roll the snake until it's stiff enough to balance on your finger like a pencil. **"It might poke your eye out!"**

6 Rinse the soap out of the wool by diving and shaking the snake in the rinse bucket, yelling **"Yeow! It's a dangerous snake!"** Squeeze out the excess water, and then, on top of a dry surface, bend the snake into nice tight curves as shown. (The curves will release slightly naturally.) Let the snake stay in this position until it's completely dry and ready to play with.

The Perfect Little Bag

Fill this bag with almost anything—your glasses, spare change, pencils, or love notes. It's also handy for keeping small tools at your fingertips during craft projects.

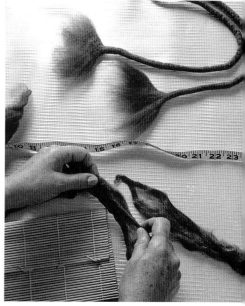

1 Divide the orange Merino wool sliver down the center, and lay it on the felt mat. Overlap the ends in the middle (see photo) to make a long strap, approximately 48 inches (121.9 cm). Roll the sliver slightly with your hands to condense the fibers. Keeping a 3-inch (7.6 cm) length dry on each end, dip the center of the wool into the wetting mix, and squeeze to saturate. Lay the wool on the felt mat, and roll it with your hands and the sushi mat (refer to instructions for Basic Felt Snakes on page 20) until it's very dense. Open out the dry wool ends into roots.

WHAT YOU NEED

Basic feltmaking kit

24-inch-long (61 cm) orange Merino wool sliver

Sushi mat

Plastic sheeting

Lightweight fabric

1 ounce (28.4 g) blue Merino wool sliver

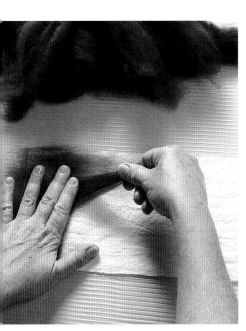

2 Measure and cut out an 8 x 6-inch (20.3 x 15.2 cm) resist pattern from the plastic sheeting. Measure and cut a 16 x 6-inch (40.6 x 15.2 cm) guide from the lightweight fabric. Lay out four layers of the blue Merino sliver on the fabric guide as shown following steps 2–7 of the Basic Flat Felt directions on page 22. Extend the wool layers 1 to 1½ inches (2.5 to 3.8 cm) over the edge of the fabric for the seams.

4 Take the prepared strap and tease out both of its dry roots into right angles. Place one root at the top right corner and along the side on the water line as shown. Place the plastic resist on the wet wool over the root end of the strap. Match the side water lines and extend the plastic about 1 inch (2.5 cm) beyond the folded top edge of the bag.

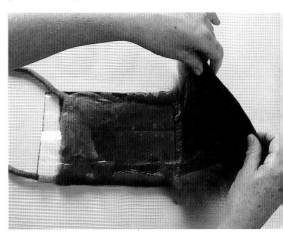

3 Flip over the batt, and remove the fabric guide. Use the wetting mix to soak only the 16 x 6-inch center of the wool. Leave the outside wool dry. At the ends of the rectangle, fold the dry wool over on the water line as shown. These will become the top edges of your bag.

5 Fold over the dry wool side seams just on the plastic resist pattern. Place the other root end of the strap along the side edge of the folded dry wool and the folded top.

6 With your thumb and forefingers, pick up the other side of the bag at the corners, and fold it over the plastic resist pattern, matching the tops.

7 Flip over the whole bag, and fold down the remaining dry wool edges onto the wet body of the bag. Follow the directions for Basic Resist Felt (page 30, steps 13 to 19) to felt and finish the bag.

The Amazing Felted Doorstop

Tired of doors that go bump in the night? Here's your amazing solution. Felt-covered stones won't scratch your floor, and you can color coordinate them with any home interior. They also make attractive paperweights.

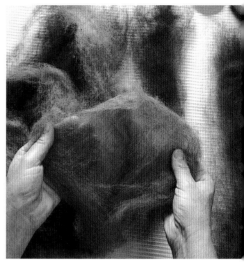

1 Tear off a section of the brown wool batt, divide it into four layers, and then divide each of those layers into four strips.

2 Take one strip of brown wool, and tightly wrap it lengthwise around a stone, overlapping the sides and ends. Holding the wool on the stone, dip it into the wetting mix. Pat the wool with your fingers to saturate. To flatten any unruly fibers, smooth on a small amount

---

WHAT YOU NEED

Basic feltmaking kit

1 ounce (28.4 g) brown Pelssau/Gotland wool blend

Round, clean stones

¼ ounce (7.1 g) gold Pelssau/Gotland wool blend

---

of the soap gel mix. Take another wool strip, and wrap it around the stone in the opposite direction (see photo). Dip the stone into the wetting mix, adding soap gel mix as needed. Wrap four more layers of wool around the stone, each in the opposite direction of the previous layer. Dip the stone into the wetting mix after each layer of wool is applied, and smooth it down with soap gel mix and your fingers.

4 Hold the stone in your hand, and slowly and gently rub one side for a minute. Turn the stone over, and rub its other side for a minute. Continue to rub and flip the stone until the felt becomes tight against the stone. Apply liberal amounts of soap gel mix to keep the wool surface lubricated.

3 Take a strip of the gold wool, and wrap it around the center of the stone as shown, overlapping the ends. Wrap the rest of the stone with strips of the brown wool. Dip the stone into the wetting mix. Apply soap gel mix as needed as you smooth down the wool. Wrap two more layers of gold wool around the middle of the stone and two more layers of brown wool on its sides, dipping and smoothing between each addition.

5 Rub the wool with more force, using your fingertips when the felt begins to feel firm. When the felt is very dense, thoroughly rinse the stone under very hot water to remove the soap. Squeeze the felted rock in a towel, and then put it in the sun to dry.

VARIATION

For additional doorstops (or paperweights), you can make up your own designs using solid colors, several stripes, half-and-half colors, or even spots.

Twist Bracelets

Make these distinctive twined bracelets in every color of your wardrobe. You can wear several at once and make dozens for special presents. The bracelets are hardened with a glue and water mixture, so they'll last a long time.

WHAT YOU NEED

Basic feltmaking kit

2 Merino wool slivers in contrasting colors, each about 30 inches (76.2 cm) long

Large bulldog clip

Sushi mat

Sewing needle and thread

Rolling pin

White craft glue

1 Divide each color of wool into two equal lengths. Use one length of each color for one bracelet. Fasten one end of each of the two slivers to the large bulldog clip, and attach the clip to something sturdy, like a tabletop. (You'll be pulling the slivers against this clip, so make sure the connection is strong.) Hold one sliver in each hand, about 6 inches (15.2 cm) from the clip. Use your thumbs and forefingers to individually and tightly twist each sliver in the same direction. When you can't twist them any further, wrap the twisted

slivers around each other in the opposite direction (see photo). This is called *plying*. Continue wrapping until you reach the end of the twisted area. Move your fingers 12 inches (30.5 cm) further down the loose part of the slivers. Continue tightly twisting the individual slivers, and then wrapping the twisted slivers around each other until you reach the end of the wool.

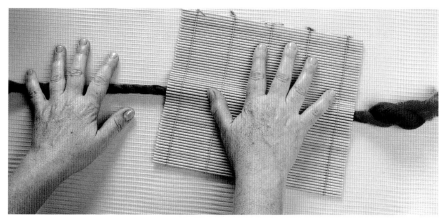

2 Remove the ends of the slivers from the clip. Holding each end, dip the plied slivers into the wetting mix, and squeeze several times to saturate the wool. Squeeze out the excess water, and place the sliver on the felt mat. Using heavy pressure, roll the plied sliver on the felt mat with your hands, and then with the sushi mat as shown. Add soap gel mix if the wool seems dry. Roll about five to eight minutes until the slivers have felted together and the twists can't be pulled apart.

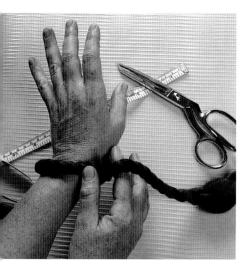

3 Cut the straggly end off the plied sliver. Wrap the bracelet around your wrist, making sure you can easily pull it on and off over your knuckles. Measure this length, and add 1 inch (2.5 cm) to the total. Measure and cut the bracelet to the correct length.

4 Use a double-threaded needle to tightly sew the bracelet ends together. Carefully match the the colors and the twist of the sliver.

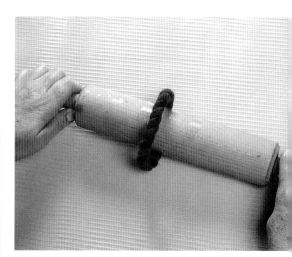

5 Dip the sewn bracelet into the soap gel, and then rub it for a minute or two to felt the sewn ends together. Place the bracelet on the rolling pin. Using a lot of pressure, roll the bracelet back and forth as shown until it shrinks to fit your arm and the sewing stitches disappear. Rinse out the soap in hot water, and squeeze the bracelet dry in a towel.

6 Prepare a mixture of ½-cup (118.2 ml) white craft glue and ½-cup water. Stir this mixture well, and then soak the bracelet in it. Squeeze out the excess glue mixture. If the bracelet has lost some of its shape, gently reroll it a few times on the rolling pin. Place the bracelet on a non-porous surface, and let dry.

Pocket Bears

Keep these dear little bears right in your pocket. They're the perfect size to fit in your hand, and they make wonderful travel companions. A traditional felted toy, I learned this project from a friend in Denmark. Adopt a whole cheerful bear family in different colors and bow ties.

1 Divide the ½ ounce (14.2 g) of Pelssau/Gotland wool into two piles. Separate one pile of wool into palm-size pieces, and set aside. Form the second pile of wool into a tight fat cigar shape that is as long as your palm. Dip the wool cigar into the wetting mix, and squeeze it several times to saturate. Add soap gel mix to the surface, and gently rub the wool cigar between your palms as shown for about four minutes until it's lightly felted and holds together.

2 Visually divide the lightly felted wool into thirds. The top third is the bear's head. Create the head by tightly wrapping and tying a short piece of buttonhole thread around the neck. Make legs for the bear by cutting the bottom third of the felted wool in half (see photo).

WHAT YOU NEED

Basic feltmaking kit
Pelssau/Gotland wool blend in various colors, ½ ounce (14.2 g) for each bear
Buttonhole thread
Embroidery floss
Sharp embroidery needle with large eye

3 Cut the arms from the sides of the bear, starting at the knee and cutting upward at an angle toward the neck as shown.

5 Use your fingertips to rub the bear with soap gel mix until the wool is very densely felted. This will take about 10 minutes. As you rub, bend out the bottoms of the bear's legs into little feet, and pinch up loose wool on top of the bear's head to form little ears (see photo).

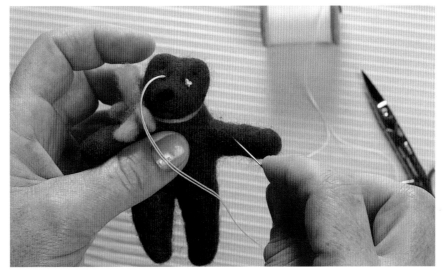

4 Wrap dry pieces of wool from the reserved pile around the legs and arms of the bear, criss-crossing the chest and back. Give the bear personality by adding small pads of wool on the stomach, buttocks, and nose areas. Secure these features by wrapping more wool around those areas. Keep adding wool until the bear looks well-proportioned. Dip the bear frequently in the wetting mix, and rub on soap gel mix to "glue" the wool down.

6 Vigorously rinse the bear under hot water, and reposition its arms and legs. Knot the ends of a double length of embroidery floss, and push the needle into the head at position 1. Come out at position 2. Pull hard on the knot to pull it inside of the felt. Continue creating a face for the bear following the numbered sequence shown in figure 1. Take a short length of dry wool, roll it between your hands with a few drops of water until it slightly felts, and then tie it around the bear's neck to make the scarf. Finish with a bow.

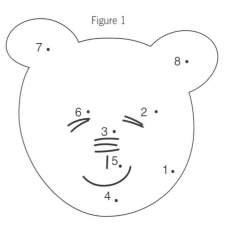

Figure 1

Here, Kitty, Kitty

You can create a life-size stuffed kitty as a playmate for your real live kitty using this unusual felting method. The basic shape of the kitty is carved from foam rubber. Its head and tail are sewn on with a needle and thread. With a little practice, you can give your kitty any lifelike position.

Note: For this project, make the wetting mix with water as hot as your hands can stand. The hot water will help the wool felt faster.

1 Cut out the photocopied pattern and use it as a guide to draw the shape of kitty body, head, and tail onto the foam rubber.

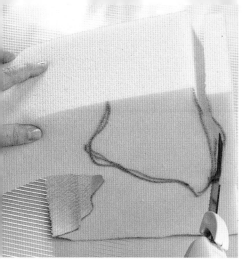

2 Cut out the kitty parts with the electric knife as shown. Sculpt the cut foam with scissors for a smooth life-like look.

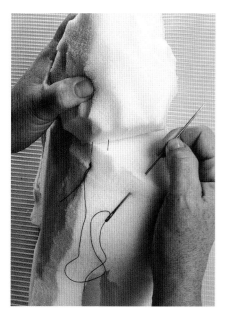

3 Turn the kitty's head to get a playful look. Securely sew the head and tail to the body with the poultry needle and thread. Tie the thread to itself. (Any knots will pull through the foam rubber.) Don't worry about the size or look of the stitches; they will be covered with felted wool.

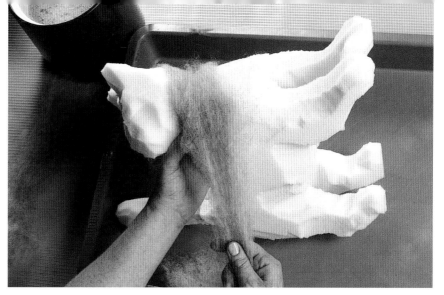

4 Divide the wool batt lengthwise into thinner strips for ease in wrapping. Wrap the main wool color around all parts of the foam kitty, crisscrossing the body when necessary. Pull the wool securely, but not so tight that the foam starts to distort.

5 Wrap another layer of wool around the kitty, and pour more wetting mix over it. Gently rub with your hands to saturate and flatten the wool. Repeat this process four or five more times, until your kitty's body is nice and smooth and plump, and all the formerly separate parts flow together. The foam rubber will absorb water, so use plenty of the wetting mix.

6 On the final wool layer, design and apply kitty markings, like white spots or dark stripes, if you wish. Gently rub the soap gel mix on the kitty's body. Work one area at a time until the wool feels secure. Alternate the rubbing with gentle squeezing. (The felting actions are almost like a kitty massage.) Continue these two felting actions until the kitty is very densely felted. As the wool felts, it shrinks and slightly compresses the foam rubber. Toss the kitty 50 times, throwing it on each side. Use the pinch test to check for doneness. Rinse the kitty in a bucket of hot water to remove the soap. Squeeze the kitty between towels; even step on her to remove most of the water, and then let her sit in the sun on a towel until dry. Remember that the foam rubber is similar to a sponge and will absorb water, so the kitty will take some time to dry. Tie a beautiful ribbon around her neck or make a necklace of felted beads. Sew on some buttons for eyes.

Miracle Bead Necklace

Whether you pair it with a T-shirt or an evening gown, this 35-inch (89 cm) necklace introduces a dramatic burst of color. Your friends will have a hard time believing that these unfuzzy and very hard beads are actually felted wool. The beads may take overnight to dry, so allow two days to finish the project.

YOU WILL NEED

Basic feltmaking kit

½ ounce (14.2 g)
black Merino wool sliver

Red, blue, yellow, orange, and white
Merino wool slivers,
each ¼ ounce (7.1 g)

Sushi mat

White craft glue

Cutting board

Sharp knife

Sharp large-eye needle to thread
beading wire

50 inches (cm) of seven strand,
nylon-coated bead stringing wire

Pliers

35 puka shell beads or white buttons

Wire cutters

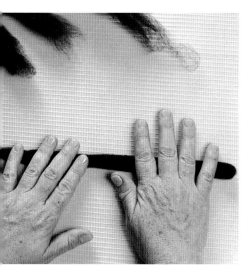

1 Take the black Merino wool sliver, and divide it lengthwise into four equal pieces. Lay one length on the felting mat, and overlap the ends of the additional divided slivers to form a 20-inch-long (50.8 cm) snake. Roll the sliver into a snake with dry hands to consolidate the wool fibers (see photo).

2 Take the red Merino wool sliver, and lay out a thin 4 x 20-inch (10.2 x 50.8 cm) rectangle of wool (similar to the snake's clothing on page 37). Place the black snake along the long edge of the red wool rectangle, and roll it up with your hands as tightly as possible. Roll the snake back and forth a few times to make it firm.

3 Repeat step 2 with each Merino wool color in this order: blue, yellow, orange, blue, black, white, black, and another black. Each time you lay out a new wool color, increase the width of the rectangle by 1 inch (2.5 cm) or more so it will fit around the growing snake. When finished, your fat snake will be about 4 inches (10.2 cm) in diameter. It also will have grown longer by 4 to 5 inches (10.2 and 12.7 cm). Roll the dry, fat snake with your hands for a minute to tighten the wool fibers.

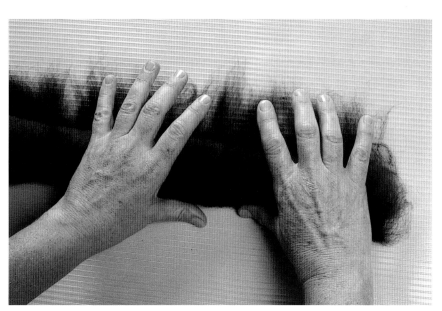

4 Use a dipper to gently pour wetting mix down the length of the snake. Press down and flatten the snake, adding more water if necessary to saturate the snake. Pinch the sides of the snake together, and carefully roll the soggy snake back and forth with your hands. If the snake seems dry, add more soap gel mix. Continue to roll the snake, increasing your hand pressure as the snake gets firmer. To speed up the felting process, use the sushi mat as shown to roll the firm snake. When complete, the snake should measure about ¾ inch (1.9 cm) in diameter and feel very stiff. Rinse the snake in hot water to remove the soap. Roll the snake in a big towel, place it on the floor, and walk on the lump to press out most of the water.

5 Mix ½-cup (118.2 ml) white craft glue with ½-cup warm water, and stir well. Soak the snake in this mixture, repeatedly squeezing to saturate. Squeeze out enough glue mixture so the snake surface doesn't look coated with white glue. Hang the snake in front of a fan overnight to dry.

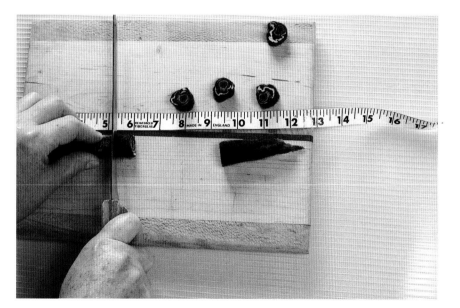

6 Place the snake on a cutting board, and lay a measuring tape along the top edge as a guide. Use the sharp knife to cut off about 2 inches (5 cm) from each end of the snake. Slice the remaining snake into 35 beads, each 1-inch (2.5 cm) long. Squeeze the bead to check for complete dryness. If the bead center oozes any white glue mixture, let the bead set until it's dry. (The beads will dry very hard because of the glue mixture.)

7 Thread the sharp large-eye needle with the beading wire. Pierce the felt beads through their sides. (You may need to use pliers to pull the needle through the bead, see photo.) Alternate stringing the puka shells or white buttons with the felt beads, ending with a puka shell. When all the beads and shells or buttons are strung, leave 3 inches (7.6 cm) of wire at both ends. Cut the wire with wire cutters, and securely tie off the beading wire. Hide the ends of the wire by threading them through the needle and pulling them through the nearest felt bead. Clip any remaining visible wire.

Marvelous Mittens

Whether you're walking the dog, driving the car, or throwing snowballs, you'll stay warm in these cheerful, cozy mittens. They make great presents, and can be sized to fit anyone. The directions are for medium-size mittens. Increase or decrease the wool amounts for smaller or larger hands.

WHAT YOU NEED

Basic feltmaking kit

10 x 15-inch (25.4 x 38.1 cm) rectangle of yellow Merino wool prefelt*

5 x 5-inch (12.7 x 12.7 cm) square of red Merino wool prefelt*

18 x 18-inch (45.7 x 45.7 cm) sheet of paper

Ruler

Plastic sheeting

2 ounces (56.7 g) blue Merino sliver

2 small water or soda bottles

*Follow the Basic Prefelt directions on page 26.

1 Cut out two stars from the yellow prefelt. Each star should measure about 4 inches (10.2 cm). Cut out two hearts from the red prefelt. Each heart should measure about 2 inches (5 cm). Cut out a long 4 x 14-inch (10.2 x 35.6 cm) rectangle of yellow prefelt for the cuff decoration. As shown, cut out a scallop border down the long sides of the rectangle.

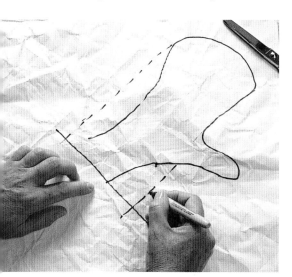

2 Place your hand down on the paper with your fingertips about 3 inches (7.6 cm) from the edge of the page. Spread your fingers apart about ½ inch (1.3 cm), and open your thumb very wide so it's almost perpendicular

to the rest of your hand. Draw around your hand down to your wrist, ending where you want the mittens to end. Look at your drawing, and make the following modifications: use the ruler to draw a line from the outside of your little finger straight down to the mitten cuff, ignoring the natural curve of your hand; draw another line (see photo) straight down from the outside of your forefinger past your thumb and to the mitten cuff. (The cuff of the mitten should be as wide as the center of your hand.) Finally, draw a cuff line.

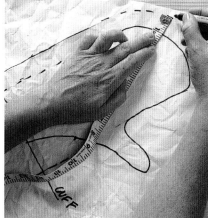

3 Draw another line 1 inch (2.5 cm) outside of the line drawn and modified in step 2 (see photo). This is your cutting line. Fold the paper in half at the cuff line, and cut along the line. You now should have two hands joined together at the cuff line with their thumbs on the same side. This is your pattern.

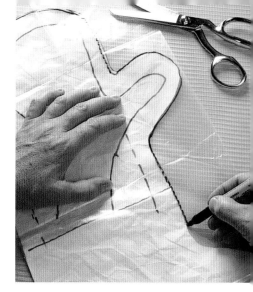

4 Place the plastic sheeting over the paper pattern, and trace as shown. Cut out the plastic resist, and lay it on the felting mat. Follow the directions for Basic Resist Felting on page 27, steps 1 through 12, but skip step 6 and step 11 (creating an opening).

Hint: When you're folding over the dry edges in the crotch of the thumb, it's easier to carefully tease apart the seam wool almost to the pattern, and then fold it over the plastic resist as shown below.

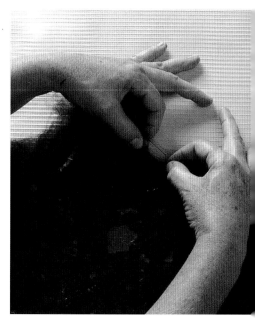

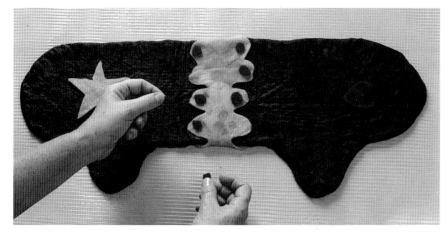

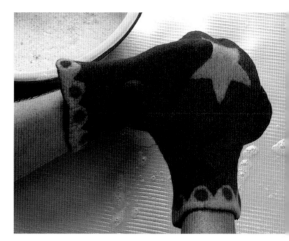

5 Place one yellow star on the back and one red heart on the palm of each mitten. Place the scalloped border exactly in the middle of the cuff area. Wrap the border around the felt, and adjust the scallops so they meet smoothly. (You may need to slightly trim where they meet.) Cut out small circles of red prefelt, and place them in the center of the scallops. Gently rub soap gel mix on the prefelt areas to help them adhere to the mittens. Follow the directions for Basic Resist Felting, step 13, until you're ready to remove the resist. Cut across the cuff line of the mittens, right down the center of the scalloped border, and remove the plastic resist.

7 Put one mitten on your right hand, and rub it with your left hand. Put the other mitten on your left hand, and rub with your right hand. Put both mittens on, and rub your hands together. The mittens will form to your hands, and you will end up with a specific right and left mitten. Continue steps 17 to 19 to rub, squeeze, and throw the mittens until they almost fit. (Don't make them fit perfectly because you still have to rinse them.) Gently rinse out the soap with cool water, and put the mittens back on your hands. (They may be a bit tight because they are wet, but you can stretch them out a little.) Carefully take the mittens off so they retain the shape of your hands, and place them over small soda or water bottles to dry.

6 To rub out the seam ridges, place your hand inside the mitten, and gently pull and rub the seam bump with soap gel mix. Concentrate on the thumb area first, felting and shrinking it almost to the finished size.

Coffee Cozy

This cheerful rooster can't wait to crow "good morning" to you as he keeps your plunge pot coffee hot and tasty. Make a whole flock to greet friends and family every day.

WHAT YOU NEED

Basic feltmaking kit

1 ounce (28.4 g) red Merino wool sliver

3 x 6-inch (7.6 x 15.2 cm) fabric resist

Photocopied chicken resist template, page 79, enlarged to 200%

Plastic sheeting

1 ounce (28.4 g) brown Pelssau/Gotland wool blend*

Small amounts of Merino wool prefelt in white, black, and yellow (see page 26)

*For this project, you'll separate the Pelssau/Gotland batt into layers, and then tear them into strips. Lay these strips down as you would Merino wool slivers.

Note: You'll use a plastic resist pattern to make the chicken body and a fabric resist to create the prefelted cockscomb. The black and white eyes and yellow beak are cut from prefelt. Read over the instructions for making prefelt (page 26), flat felt (page 22), and resist felt (page 27) before starting.

Note: This coffee cozy fits an individual-serving-size plunge pot. If you wish to make a coffee cozy for a larger or smaller container, make a resist pattern by drawing a rectangle on the plastic sheeting with the following measurements. Measure the circumference of your container, divide the number in half, and then add 1 inch (2.5 cm). This is the width of the pattern. Measure from the center top of your pot to the bottom. Add 1 inch to this number. This is the height of your pattern. Draw the rectangle, and add the beak area as shown on the pattern, curving the top of the cozy to follow the shape of your coffeepot.

1 To make the cockscomb, lay out four layers of the red Merino wool in a 5 x 5-inch (12.7 x 12.7 cm) square. Place the fabric resist over the lower half of the wool, extending the resist about ½ inch (1.3 cm) beyond the bottom and sides of the wool. Place another four layers of the red Merino wool over the entire batt(see photo). Fold over any wool fibers that extend from the edge of the batt. Wet the batt with the wetting mixture.

4 Transfer the photocopied chicken body template onto plastic, and cut out. Follow the directions for Basic Resist Felt on page 27 using the Pelssau/Gotland wool blend. Complete steps 1 through 12 for the wetting of the chicken body. For steps 6 and 11, create an opening at the bottom of the chicken body.

2 Felt the entire cockscomb batt following the instructions for Basic Flat Felt on page 22 until the wool gets to the soft felt or prefelt stage (step 13). Continue to rub only the top of the cockscomb (where there is no resist) until it's very hard and dense. Felt right to the edge of the resist fabric. Open up the prefelted layers, and remove the resist cloth. You may need to cut along the sides and bottom of the prefelt to get the fabric out.

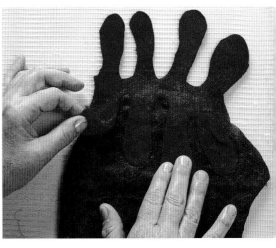

5 Before you start to press and rub the wet felt, add the cockscomb to the chicken body. Lay the prepared cockscomb on the felt mat with the top prefelt layer folded up, and the bottom prefelt layer spread out. Pick up the chicken body and place its head as close to the inside prefelt fold as possible. Bend the cockscomb to fit the curve of the head. Fold the top prefelt layer down over the chicken, and arrange the design.

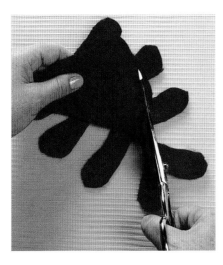

3 Cut out a cockscomb pattern from the hard-felted top as shown. Make sure that you don't cut into the prefelted layers. With the two prefelt layers together, cut them into the scalloped design.

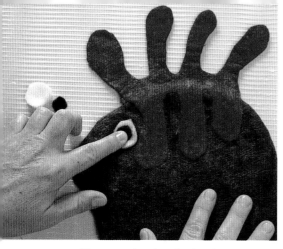

6 To make the chicken's eyes, cut two ¾-inch (1.9 cm) circles out of white Merino wool prefelt. Place one circle on the chicken's head. Cut two smaller circles for the pupils from the black Merino wool prefelt, and place one in the center of the applied white wool. Gently rub some soap gel mix on one eye for a minute to help it attach to the chicken body.

8 Felt the chicken cozy following the Basic Resist Felt instructions on page 30, steps 13 through 19. Once you've removed the plastic resist and smoothed down the seams, cut the back side of the chicken cozy 4 inches (10.2 cm) up from the bottom edge. This cut allows access to the coffeepot handle. Continue to felt, checking the size of the cozy against the coffeepot before and after the squeezing and throwing (steps 18 and 19).

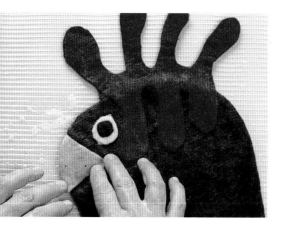

9 When the cozy is slightly larger than the coffeepot, put the cozy on the pot and trim the bottom hem. Rub the cut hem with your fingers and soap gel until it becomes rounded and matches the cozy's other felted edges. Rinse the cozy with cool water, and squeeze dry. Straighten the comb and chicken, gently forming the felt to fit the pot. Let the cozy dry on the coffeepot. Using the cockscomb as a handle, the cozy should move on and off the press pot with ease.

7 To make the chicken's beak, cut a long diamond shape from a 2 x 4-inch (5 x 10.2 cm) piece of yellow Merino wool prefelt. Center it on the pointy beak area of the chicken with the long diamond ends forming the "smile" of the beak. Flip the cozy over, and press down the other side of the prefelt beak, molding it to fit. Add some soap gel mix, and gently massage both sides of the beak. Attach the second eye to the chicken, and gently rub it with soap gel.

Fuzzy Pumpkin Throw

Curl up and enjoy chilly autumn evenings under this soft lap-size felted throw. It's our basic flat felt sampler, simply larger. Clear a big work table, and prepare to add a little flair to your favorite chair.

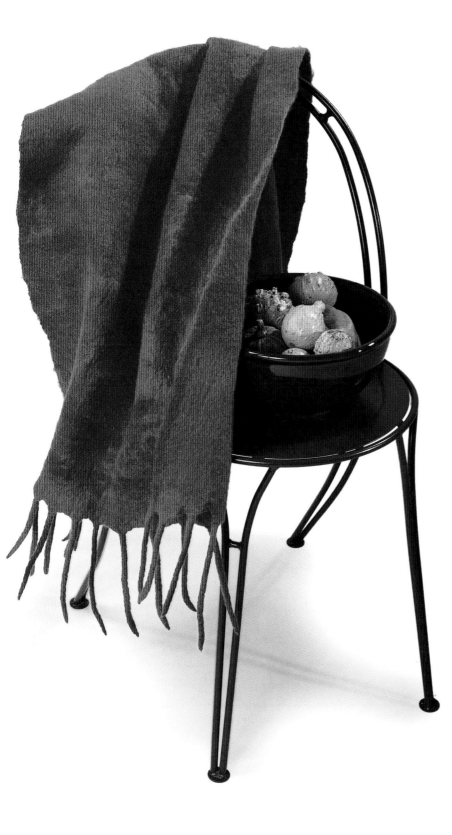

WHAT YOU NEED

Basic felting kit

16-ounces (453.6 g)of pumpkin-colored Merino wool sliver

2 large plastic felting mats, each 5 x 2 feet (152.4 x 61 cm)

Nonskid mat to fit under large felting mat

Sushi mat

Iron

Pet brush with wire teeth

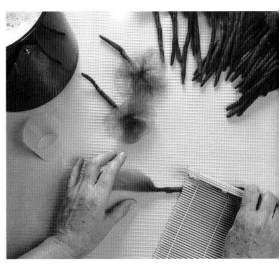

1 Take several lengths of Merino sliver, and divide them lengthwise into four equal pieces. Tear the divided sliver into 36 pieces, each 8 inches (20.3 cm) long. Keeping 2 inches (5 cm) of one end dry, follow the Basic Felt Snake instructions (dreadlock variation) on page 21. After felting, fan out the dry wool ends in a circle like the roots of a tree. Divide the remaining wool into four piles, one for each layer.

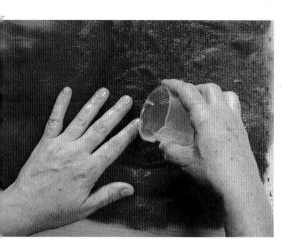

2 Following the flat felt directions on page 22, lay out four layers of wool for the throw in a 36 x 60-inch (91.4 x 152.4 cm) rectangle. Gently fold over any thin strands of wool that stick out beyond the edge of the batt. Wet down the wool with the wetting mixture as shown until it is saturated.

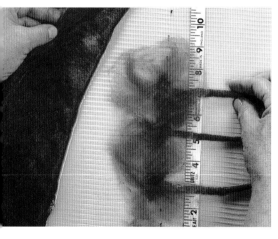

3 When the wool is saturated, attach the prepared fringe. Draw a line on the felting mat with a waterproof marker along the narrow edge of the throw. Turn back about 2 inches (5 cm) of the wet wool. Take 18 pieces of the prepared fringe, open out the dry root end into a circle, and then place them, evenly spaced, along the marker line. Make sure the inside of the root circle is turned upwards and flattened.

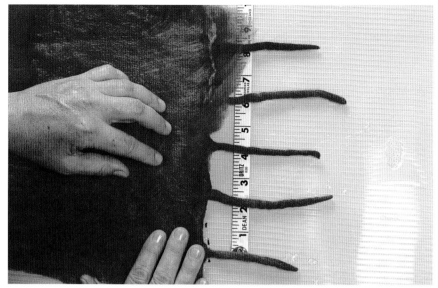

4 Pick up the pulled-back wet wool, and place it on top and over half of the fringe's root circles. Press the other half of the root circle down onto the top surface of the throw (see photo). Gently rub the edge of the throw with a small amount of the soap gel mix. Repeat steps 3 and 4 on the other end of the throw.

5 To continue felting the throw, follow the Basic Flat Felt directions, steps 10–13, on page 24. This is a large project, so take your time pressing and rubbing the wool until it passes the pinch-test stage. It helps to work a smaller area, about 2 x 2 feet (61 x 61 cm) at a time. Remove excess water from the body of the felt by pressing gently with a sponge. Slowly rub and move the felt gently up and down against the ridges on the plastic mat, bunching the felt in folds like the wrinkles on a Chinese Shar-Pei dog. When the throw is all gathered together, turn it 180°, spread it out flat, and gently rub and bunch the felt together again. Add more wetting mix to the felt if its fibers start sticking to your hands.

6   Pick up the felt, put it in the large water bucket, and squeeze it for five minutes like you're washing clothes. Gently squeeze out excess water, and then throw the felt about 75 times until it's 25 x 50 inches (63.5 x 127 cm), nearly the finished size. Rinse the felt with cool water to shrink it to the desired size of 24 x 48 (61 x 121.9 cm).

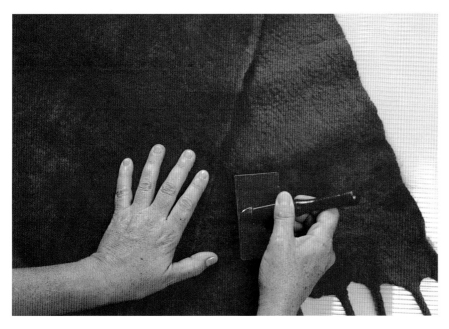

7   Iron the throw flat with a steam iron, and pull on the edges to make them straight. Hold the end of each fringe, and pull to straighten. Hang the throw over a drying rack, shower curtain rod, or clothesline until dry. Gently brush both sides of the throw and the fringe with the pet brush as shown. Use short, uplifting strokes to create a fuzzy surface.

Journal Cover

Every time you curl up to write in your journal, you'll be soothed
by the warm and textured surface of this unique book cover.
It can be made to fit any size book. The front has a pocket into
which the front cover of your book or journal slides. The felt
wraps around the book and fastens on the overlap.
This example has a felt button and loop closure, but it's fun
to invent other ways to secure the cover.

Basic feltmaking kit

2¼ ounces (63.8 g) white Merino wool sliver for button and journal

½ ounce (14.2 g) black Merino wool sliver for loop and journal

White craft glue

8 x 5½ x ¾-inch (20.3 x 14 x 1.9 cm) journal, notebook, or book*

Measuring tape

Calculator

Pattern fabric, about ½ yd (18 cm)

Iron

Clothes hanger

Black extra-wide, double-fold bias binding

Straight pins

Sewing machine

Small white button

Sewing needle and white buttonhole thread

* For making a larger or smaller journal cover, see step 3 to determine the size of your fabric pattern guide.

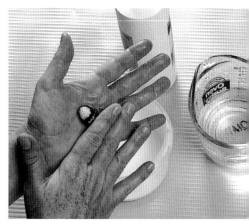

1 Make a 1-inch (2.5 cm) felt ball from the white Merino wool. Follow the directions on page 18 for the Basic Felt Ball. Just before you start to roll the ball

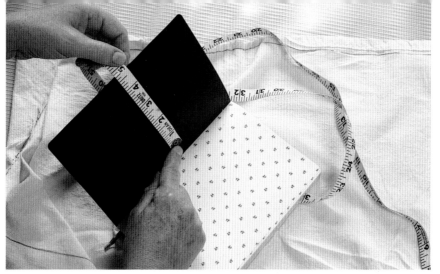

between your hands, wrap a thin strip of black Merino wool around the white ball. When the ball becomes densely felted, flatten and rub it between your hands in one direction to make an oval button (see photo). Rinse and squeeze dry in a towel. Dip and saturate the button in a solution of equal parts glue and water; squeeze out some of the glue mix; and let dry.

2 Make a loop for the closure by dividing the black sliver into four equal sections. Lay down 8 inches (20.3 cm) of the quartered sliver. Slightly roll the sliver to condense the fibers. Keeping 2 inches (5 cm) on each end dry, soak the center of the sliver in the wetting mix. Lay the sliver on the felt mat, and roll the wet center with your hands until it becomes very dense (see photo). Open up the dry ends like the roots of a tree.

3 Measure your closed book around the center; then add 4 inches (10.2 cm) for the front pocket and 4 inches for the overlap. Measure the height of the book's front cover, and add 1 inch (2.5 cm) for the seams. To determine the size of the fabric pattern guide, multiply these measurements by the shrinkage rate of 40 percent; then, add this figure back to the original measurements. Measure, mark, and cut out a rectangle pattern from the fabric according to the dimensions you've determined.

Example: The circumference of my book is 13 inches (33 cm). Add 8 inches (20.3 cm) for the pocket and overlap to get 21 inches (53.3 cm). The height is 8 inches (20.3 cm). Add 1 inch for the seams to get 9 inches (22.9 cm). This means the finished size of the felted cover will be 21 x 9 inches. To figure the shrinkage, multiply each measurement by 40 percent and add this figure back to the original number.

21 inches (53.3 cm) x 40% = 8.4 inches (21.3 cm) + 21 inches = 29.4 inches (round up to 30 inches) (74.6 cm, round up to 75 cm)
9 inches (22.9 cm) x 40% = 3.6 inches (9.2 cm) + 9 inches = 12.6 inches (32 cm)

4 Follow the directions for Basic Flat Felt on page 22, using the fabric pattern as your guide to lay out the wool sliver. Use the black sliver for the first layer and the white sliver for the second, third, and fourth (top) layers. The top layer is the outside of the cover. Flip the wool batt over and remove the fabric pattern. Fold over any loose fibers onto the batt, and continue to follow the instructions for Basic Flat Felt.

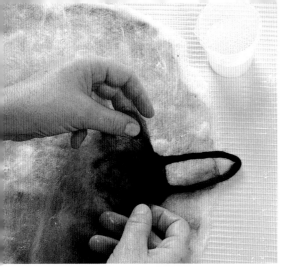

5 When you arrive at step 9, add the felted loop to one end of the top layer as shown. Rub soap gel mix on your hands and gently rub the loop roots for about two minutes. Continue to follow the directions for Basic Flat Felt through step 15. Frequently measure the cover. Rub and pull the edges to keep the rectangle even. When your felt is slightly larger than the finished size, gently rinse out the soap with cold water, and iron the felt flat with a steam iron. Trim the end with the loop closure into a nice oval shape. Hang the felt over a clothes hanger until dry.

7 Place the journal on the felt cover, and check the top and bottom fit. Trim the edges if they are uneven or if they are longer than ½ inch (1.3 cm) from the edge of the journal. It may help to measure and draw a line with ruler and marker as shown. Pin the top and bottom seams of the front pocket so the journal slides in and out smoothly.

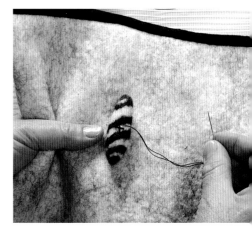

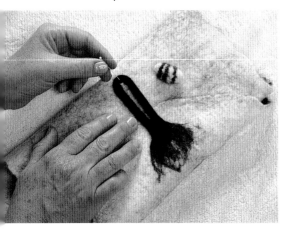

6 Wrap the dry felt around the journal as it will appear when finished. Increase or decrease the depth of the pocket so the loop end overlaps the front cover as shown. Mark that spot with a pin or thread for later button placement.

8 With right sides together, pin the bias binding around the edge of the journal cover as shown from the top corner of the front pocket around to the bottom corner of the front pocket. Extend the binding 1 inch (2.5 cm) for the seam. (You'll be stitching the edge of the pocket as well as the binding tape.) Use a sewing machine to stitch on the binding with a ⅜-inch (9.5 mm) seam. Turn the binding to the inside, and use a blind stitch to sew it down by hand.

9 Place the felt cover on the journal and readjust the button placement if necessary. Using a doubled buttonhole thread, sew on the felt button at the same time you sew on the small regular button inside the journal cover. This helps prevent the button thread from pulling through the felt. Fasten the loop around the button.

Sweet Snuggle Slippers

Imagine a cozy evening around the fireplace, snow falling outside, and everyone wearing cheerfully colored slippers. Make these delightful foot warmers with leather bottoms, so you can wear them safely on all floor surfaces without slipping.

Note: The wool amounts listed are for a fairly thin, flexible, women's size 8 (European size 38) slipper. Adjust the amount of wool for bigger or smaller feet, and just follow the directions for laying out Basic Resist Felt on page 27 with four thin even layers of wool. If you have cold feet, make thicker layers of wool.

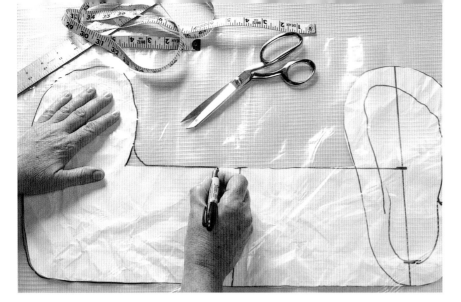

1 Step on the paper with your bare foot about 4 inches (10.2 cm) away from one edge. Trace your foot with the marker. Remove your foot. Draw another line 1 inch (2.5 cm) outside of your traced foot pattern. Draw a center line straight down the length of your foot pattern. Mark the center of the foot and the heel. Look at your pattern and imagine the side of a boot. Make the sides of the boot by drawing two 9-inch (22.9 cm) parallel lines from the center mark on the foot and the back of the heel. Draw a line across the top of the boot. Fold the paper in half at this center line. With the paper doubled, cut out the boot pattern along the outside line. You now have a pattern of two slipper boots joined at the top opening, or cuff. Trace this paper pattern on the plastic sheeting as shown. Cut out the plastic to use as the resist pattern. (Making both slippers at once saves a lot of time.)

3 Continue following the directions for Basic Resist Felt. You won't be creating an opening in the slipper, so skip step 6 and step 11. Remember that the mixed-color layer goes on the outside of your slippers. Remove the resist at step 14 by cutting across the center cuff line with scissors. Rub a little soap gel mix on the cut edges, and massage for a minute to prevent stretching. Reach into the slipper, grab the resist by the toe, and pull it out as shown. Continue following the directions for Basic Resist Felt, throwing the slippers about 50 times for step 19. (You can reuse the plastic resist pattern to make more slippers; just tape it back together at the cuff line.)

2 Divide all the wool colors into two equal piles, one pile for each side. Following the directions for Basic Resist Felt on page 27, use the blue wool for the first three layers on each side of the pattern. As you lay out the fourth layer, start with the purple Merino wool sliver at the toe; mix in the green sliver for the body of the slipper; then finish with the blue wool at the cuff. The colors will blend together as they are felted.

4 Try on the slippers. Stand on a towel, and check the size. Sit down and start to shrink the slipper to your exact foot size by rubbing the heel area with soap gel mix. Rub the felt until it cups nicely around your heel as shown. Next, squeeze the slipper against your foot, rubbing and shrinking the arch area with more soap gel mix. The direction you rub your hand is the direction the wool will felt and shrink more. Continue to squeeze and rub the felt until the slipper is slightly larger than your foot when you stand up. (Don't walk around in the sudsy slippers because they are very slippery.) Keep the cuff opening above your ankle larger to get your foot in and out.

5 Take off the slippers, and gently rinse them in cool water to remove the soap. Wipe the soap off your feet, and put the slippers back on. Because the lubricating soap has been rinsed out, this will be harder to do. Just work patiently, trying not to stretch the felt. If you're having trouble, stretch the instep with your hands. (Note that the slippers have shrunk to fit either your right or left foot, and make sure they go back on the correct one.) Pat the slippers with your hands to fit them against your foot. Very gently slide the slippers back off, reform the slippers back to your foot shape, and place them upright on a towel to dry.

6 Measure, pin, and machine-stitch the binding to the outside of the cuffs. Fold the binding to the inside and hand-stitch. The slippers can be worn with the cuffs up or folded down.

Making Your Own Leather Soles

Trace the outside of your foot onto a piece of flat leather. Draw another line 1½ inches (3.8 cm) outside of the first line, and cut out the soles. Sew a running stitch along the edge of the leather, and place the slipper (with your foot inside) on the leather sole. Pull up the running stitch so the leather sole gathers around the slipper. Tie off the running stitch to keep this measurement. Pin the bias tape, right sides together, to the gathered edge. Machine-stitch, fold the bias tape inside, and then hand-stitch the bias tape's center fold to the slipper. Repeat this process for the other slipper.

Hugs and Kisses Beret

This stylish hat provides just the right amount of warmth on chilly days. Featuring bold and bright prefelt designs and a jolly dreadlock which can be knotted or not, this bright yellow beret brings a kiss of sunshine to everyone.

WHAT YOU NEED

Basic feltmaking kit
Plastic sheeting
Ruler
6 x 6-inch (15.2 x 15.2 cm) square red Merino wool prefelt (see page 26)
6 x 6-inch (15.2 x 15.2 cm) square blue Merino wool prefelt (see page 26)
2 ounces (56.7 g) yellow Merino wool sliver
Cardboard circle, 5 inches (12.7 cm) in diameter
Iron

Note: You can make this beret with a 12-, 14-, or 16-inch (30.5, 35.6, or 40.6 cm) diameter. The 5-inch (12.7 cm) head hole stays the same, but the larger the outside circumference of the beret, the floppier it becomes. Increase or decrease wool amounts for different diameters. These amounts are for a 14-inch (35.6 cm) diameter beret.

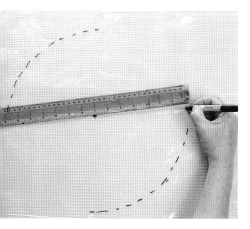

1 To make the plastic resist pattern, draw a 14-inch (35.6 cm) circle on the plastic sheeting. To do this, mark a center spot, and then use a ruler to measure and mark 7 inches (17.8 cm) from that spot. Move the ruler in a circle, and mark a series of 7-inch measurements as shown. Draw a line connecting the marks, cut out the plastic, and place it on the felting mat.

2 Measure and cut apart the 6 x 6-inch (15.2 x 15.2 cm) red and blue prefelt squares into 2 x 2-inch (5 x 5 cm) blocks. Cut nine Xs and nine Os from the red and blue blocks.

3 Divide a 9-inch (22.9 cm) yellow Merino wool sliver into four equal lengths. Using one length, follow the Basic Felt Snake directions on page 20 to make a dreadlock. Remember to leave a 2-inch (5 cm) dry root end and pull it open into a circle.

4 Divide the rest of the yellow Merino wool into two piles, one for each side. Lay out three layers of the yellow wool following the directions for Basic Resist Felt on page 27. On the fourth layer, lay out the wool in a pattern that radiates from the center point to the edges. Lay out both sides of the beret this way. When you assemble the beret to felt it, place the first wool batt with the radiating layer down on the felting mat. When you place the second side of the beret, make sure the radiating layer is on top of the wool batt. There is no opening to create, so skip step 6 and step 11. Continue to follow the directions for Basic Resist Felt through step 12.

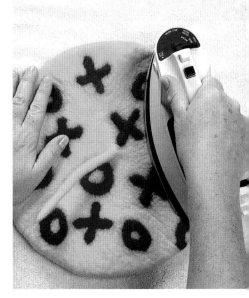

5 Before starting step 13 of Basic Resist Felt, add the dreadlock root to the center of the beret top as shown. Place nine prefelt designs equal distances from each other around the dreadlock. Drape four prefelt designs halfway over the outside edge of the beret. Rub some soap gel mix on your hands, and then gently rub both the root of the dreadlock and the prefelts for about three minutes until they attach to the beret. Carefully flip over the beret, and fold down the draped prefelt designs around the edge. Arrange the remaining five prefelt designs, keeping clear a 5-inch (12.7 cm) diameter circle in the center of the hat. Put more soap gel mix on your hands, and gently rub the prefelt designs for three minutes. Continue following the Basic Resist Felt directions until step 14.

6 Center the cardboard circle pattern on the bottom side of the beret, and carefully cut around it as shown. Don't cut through the plastic resist inside the beret. This is your head opening. Pull out the plastic resist. To keep the cut edge from stretching, rub a little soap gel mix on it for about a minute. Continue the Basic Resist Felt instructions through step 19. Throw the beret about 50 times.

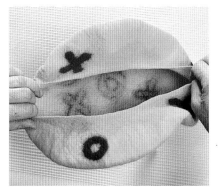

7 Gently rinse out the soap with cool water. Try the beret on your head or the head of the intended wearer. If the opening is too small, place your hands at opposite sides of the opening as shown and gently pull. Move your hands around the opening, giving a small pull each time. Be careful as this action can quickly increase the size of the head opening. Enlarge the opening until the fit is comfortable. If the head opening is too big, soak the beret in the wetting mix and throw a few more times. Vigorously rinse the beret under hot water to shrink it more.

8 Place the beret on a towel, and iron both sides to smooth the felt. Holding the base of the dreadlock, pull hard on the other end to straighten. Hang the beret over a clothesline to dry.

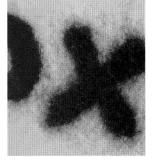

Note: If it looks like the red and blue dyes in your prefelt designs are running onto the yellow wool, take a closer look. The individually dyed wool fibers are really just mixing along the edges of the design. Sometimes this produces nice optical effects.

Note: If a piece of prefelt just doesn't want to stick to your project, ignore it during the felting process. Don't try to lift it off or poke at it.

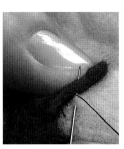

When your project is finished, simply sew down the loose prefelt with a needle and matching thread.

Double Puzzle Table Runner

Make a stunning table runner using a positive/negative pattern designed to fool the eye. Prefelted pattern pieces are hand-stitched together and then felted again with more wool, creating a sturdy mat to protect your tabletops. This runner takes a bit more time to complete, but the sharp, clear designs are absolutely worth it.

WHAT YOU NEED

Basic feltmaking kit

Photocopied design template, page 79

6 x 18 inches (15.2 x 45.7 cm) red prefelted Merino wool, cut into three 6 x 6-inch squares*

6 x 18 inches gold prefelted Merino wool, cut into three 6 x 6-inch squares*

Straight pins

Curved manicure scissors

42 x 15-inch (106.7 x 38.1 cm) piece of cardboard

18 x 18 inches black prefelted Merino wool, cut into six 3 x 18-inch (7.6 x 45.7 cm) strips*

Sewing needle and black thread

3 ounces (85 g) black Merino wool sliver

Iron

Razor

*The red and gold prefelts each need about 1 ounce (28.2 g) of wool. They can be laid out in a 11 x 25-inch (27.9 x 63.5 cm) wool batt. Figure on 30 percent shrinkage for these prefelts. The black border needs about 1½ ounces (42.5 g) of wool, and can be laid out in a 24 x 24-inch (61 cm x 61 cm) wool batt.

1 Cut out the center A of the photocopied design template. Pin together one red and one gold prefelt square along their edges as shown, using three pins on each side.

2 Place the A template in the center of the pinned prefelt squares, and carefully pin it down following the pinning diagram. (It's important to securely pin everything before cutting to avoid any slippage.) Use very sharp, curved manicure scissors to accurately cut out the pinned prefelt (see photo).

3 Carefully unpin the two cut prefelt squares; lay them next to each other; and switch the centers as shown. To help the centers fit nicely in their new squares, keep all the felt pieces facing the same directions when you cut them out and lay them down. This is like a jigsaw puzzle. Repeat steps 1 and 2 with all the remaining prefelt squares. When finished, place all six squares in a row on a large piece of cardboard for ease of handling and sewing.

4 Use the 3 x 18-inch (7.6 x 45.7 cm) strips of black prefelt to create a border around the center design squares. If a black strip isn't long enough, overlap its end with another strip, and then cut through both layers with scissors. Remove excess prefelt, and butt the strip ends together as shown.

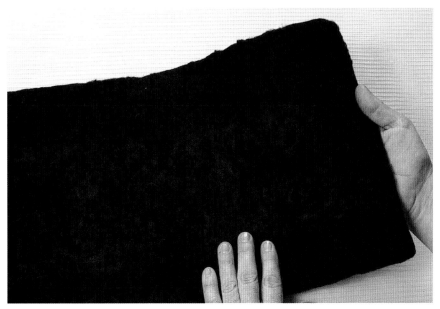

5 Sew all the prefelt seams together with a needle and single thread. Take a stitch through the prefelt about ¼ inch (6 mm) from the edge, and tie the thread to itself (any knots would pull through the loose prefelt). Then use this simple stitch: stitch down ¼ inch from the edge of one side of the seam; pull the needle back up ¼ inch on the other side of the seam; and then cross over the seam and stitch down again. Pull the stitches tight enough to hold the seams without any gaps. Make about three to four stitches per 1 inch (2.5 cm). It may help to pin some of the pieces to the cardboard so they won't move while you work. Securely stitch all pieces together.

6 Place the table runner face down on the felting mat. Lay out three perpendicular layers of black sliver on the back (see Basic Flat Felt on page 22 for directions on laying out the wool sliver). Follow the Basic Flat Felt instructions (steps 8–13) for wetting and felting the runner. You'll felt the back side first. The wool sliver laid on the back may spread out and extend beyond the prefelted black border while you felt. If needed, you can trim this edge just before step 14, throwing the runner. When you cut the felt at this step, it has a time to "heal" the cut edges, making them rounded and smooth. Continue to felt the runner until the top design layer can be seen coming through to the backside as shown, the entire runner feels sturdy, and it passes the pinch test.

7 Finish the table runner by pressing it flat with an iron. Straighten its edges by pulling and pushing and adding steam if needed. Hang the runner over a clothes hanger until dry. The stitches have become part of the felt and do not need to be removed. To clarify the design edges, use a razor to gently shave the table runner (see photo).

Airy Fairy Scarf

This lightweight yet durable felted scarf makes an impressive fashion statement. You can wear it year-round in countless ways—over the shoulders of your favorite party dress, wrapped around your neck in wintery weather, or curled up turban-like on your head.

WHAT YOU NEED

Basic feltmaking kit

7-foot-long (2.1 m) plastic felting mat

7-foot-long (2.1 m) nonskid mat

Blue, purple, and black Merino wool slivers, each 1 ounce (28.4 g)

Iron

Clothesline

Note: Before felting, the laid-out wool batt is 75 x 24 inches (190.5 x 61 cm). The finished scarf is 58 x 16 inches (147.3 x 40.6 cm).

1 The slivers are divided into very thin lengths that look as if they will barely hold together, but don't worry. The wool looks more delicate than it is. If you divide each color of wool just before you start to lay it down, it will be much easier to keep track of all the pieces. Take the black Merino wool sliver, and divide it in half lengthwise. Further divide one of those slivers in half. Keep dividing until you've halved the sliver a total of six times. The final thickness of this sliver should be about half a pencil width in diameter (see photo). We'll call this size a *pencil sliver*.

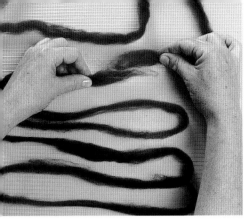

be about 1 inch (2.5 cm) apart. Turn the corners as directed in step 2. Switch to the blue pencil sliver, lay out 25 rows, and then finish with 25 rows of the purple pencil sliver. Use a dipper cup to very carefully dribble the wetting mix along each horizontal and vertical row of pencil sliver. Starting at one end of the scarf, pat down the wool with your fingers as shown to totally saturate the fibers. Add more wetting mix if the wool is still dry or if the fibers stick to your fingers.

2 Starting with the black pencil sliver, lay a 75-inch (190.5 cm) strip down the long edge of the felting mat. If the pencil sliver tears or is too short, simply lay down another piece of wool as shown, overlapping the ends. Once you reach the end of the 75-inch row, turn the sliver in a loop, and continue to lay it down toward the other end. Lay down eight rows of the black pencil sliver. Switch to the blue pencil sliver, and make another eight rows. Finish with the purple sliver for an additional eight rows. The centers of each sliver should be about 1 inch (2.5 cm) apart. To change wool colors, lay the beginning of the next color over the end of the last color.

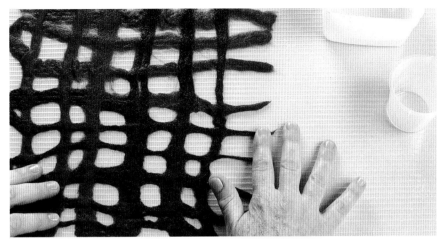

4 Check over the whole scarf, and open up the holes as needed by pushing the wool fibers back against the slivers. Rub soap gel mix onto the palms of your hands, and very lightly rub your hands in a circular motion over the wool slivers. Start at one end and rub across the surface of the scarf for about five minutes. Rub in 18 to 24-inch (45.7 to 61 cm) increments until the scarf shrinks about 3 inches (7.6 cm) in width.

5 When the felt passes the pinch test (see page 25, step 13), spread out your fingers, and use your whole hand to gently rub the felt against the ridges of the felting mat. Slowly push the scarf up as shown, making fat wrinkles like those on a Chinese Shar-Pei dog. When the scarf is all wrinkled, turn it 180 degrees, and open it out flat.
Repeat the Shar-Pei rub in this direction until the scarf is again gathered together. Pick up the whole scarf, and gently press the excess water into the rinse bucket. Squeeze the felt for about two minutes, dipping it into the rinse water after every squeeze. Following step 14 on page 25, throw the scarf about 35 to 60 times. Frequently measure the scarf as you work. When it's almost the finished size, about 17 x 60 inches (43.2 x 152.4 cm), rinse out the soap under cool water. Stretch out the scarf on a towel, pull open any closed holes, and steam iron. Straighten the scarf's edges by gently pulling them out or pushing them in as you iron. Let dry.

3 Take a black pencil sliver, and lay 25 vertical strips across and on top of the rows created in step 2. The centers of each sliver should

Hand-Quilted Pillow

Here's a truly one-of-a-kind designer pillow. The hand-felted surface is changed by the hand-quilting. You can find examples of stitching over felt on many historic and traditional felted rugs as the stitches help strengthen the felt. It's a very beautiful accent for any living room.

Basic feltmaking kit

2 squares white commercial felt, each
18 x 18 inches (45.7 x 45.7 cm)

3 ounces (85.1 g) white Merino wool
made into a 26 x 26-inch (66 x 66 cm)
batt; then felted into a 18 x 18-inch
(45.7 x 45.7 cm) square following
the Basic Flat Felt
directions on pages 22–26

White buttonhole thread

Sharp needle with large eye

T-square or carpenter's square

Blue tailor's chalk

3 ounces (85.1 g) black Merino wool
made into a 26 x 26-inch (66 x 66 cm)
batt; then felted into a 18 x 18-inch
(45.7 x 45.7 cm) square following the
Basic Flat Felt directions
on pages 22–26

Sewing machine

Buttons (optional)

Black buttonhole thread (optional)

28-inch-long (71.1 cm) Merino wool
slivers, 1 white and 1 black

Bulldog clip

Sewing needle and black thread for
basting stitches and attaching edging

Pillow stuffing or 14 x 14-inch (35.6 x
35.6 cm) commercial pillow form

Stitching Tips

•Use big knots so the thread tension doesn't pull the knot through the felt, or tie the ending thread to the beginning of the next.

• Maintaining tension on the thread is important in creating surface texture.

• To avoid discomfort, you may want to wear a flexible adhesive bandage where you pull the thread against your hand.

• Roll up the part of the pillow you're not working on for easier handling.

• Place the pillow cover on a piece of cardboard while stitching to help support the felt.

•Use a single buttonhole thread in small lengths about 36 inches (91.4 cm) long.

• Make about four to five stitches per 1 inch (2.5 cm).

• Stitches that are ¼ to ⅜ inch (6 to 9.5 mm) in length are the best to use. Smaller stitches give you less dimensionality in your quilting.

• Sew each stitch one at a time, not as a running stitch. Push the needle through all three layers, pull the thread tight, and then push the needle back through to the surface, and pull tight again.

This is the stitching pattern for this pillow sample.

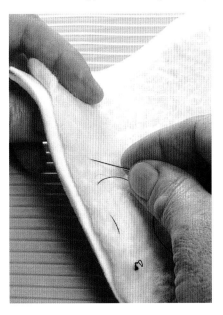

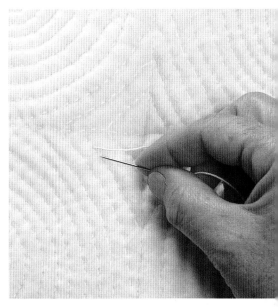

1 Place two sheets of the commercial felt under the white handmade felt square. Using a running stitch, baste along the edge with sewing thread to hold all the felt layers together.

2 Using a T-square or carpenter's square, draw a light line with the tailor's chalk 1 inch (2.5 cm) from the edge of the felt. Measure and draw another border line 2 inches (5 cm) inside the first line. Measure and divide the center area into four equal sections. Quilt along all the blue chalk lines. Quilt another line ¼ inch (6 mm) inside both sides of the border lines. Remove the basting stitches.

Starting at the center of each square, quilt a spiral as shown without drawing a chalk line. The pillow has more interest if each spiral is a little different. Fill up the corners by quilting partial curves of the spiral, matching the curves with the neighboring square.

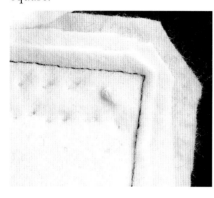

3 On the back of the stitched felt, grade the seams of the commercial felts as shown by trimming the seam of the inner felt layer to ¼ inch (6 mm) from the first stitched line and slightly more from the seam of the outer felt layer. (This makes turning the pillow cover inside out much easier.)

4 Cut the black felt in half, forming two 12 x 18-inch (30.5 x 45.7 cm) sections. With the right sides together, match up and pin the black felt to the white stitched felt, overlapping the extra black felt in the center back of the pillow. (This is the opening for the pillow form or stuffing.) Slowly machine-stitch all sides of the pillow just outside the first quilting line. This is very thick material, so use a heavy needle. Trim the corners, and then turn the pillow cover right side out by pulling through the back opening.

If you want to put buttons and buttonholes on the back overlap, use two flat buttons and cut two slits for the buttonholes. Reinforce the holes with a buttonhole stitch as shown.

5 To make the twined edging, you'll need a 28-inch (71.1 cm) long piece of both white and black Merino wool slivers. Divide each color into four equal sections. Working with one color, lay down the divided sliver on the felt mat, overlapping the ends until you have a long sliver, approximately 110 inches (279.4 cm). Sprinkle wetting mix over the sliver, and roll it slightly with your hands to consolidate the fibers. Pour on more wetting mix to saturate the fibers. Roll the wet soapy wool with your hands until the sliver becomes a dense, skinny snake. Repeat this process with the second wool color.

6 Fasten one end of each of the two snakes to a bulldog-type clip. Attach the clip to something sturdy like a tabletop. (You'll be pulling the snakes against this clip, so make sure it's a strong connection.) Hold one snake in each hand, about 6 inches (15.2 cm) from the clip. Use your thumbs and forefingers to separately and tightly twist each snake in the same direction. When you can't twist them any further, wrap the twisted snakes around each other in the opposite direction (see photo). Continue wrapping until you reach the end of the twisted area. Move your fingers 12 inches (30.5 cm) further along the loose snakes, and repeat the twisting and the wrapping until you reach the end of the loose snake. Knot both ends.

7 Hand-stitch the twined edging along the edge of the pillow, hiding the seam. Let the excess 2 to 3 inches (5 to 7.6 cm) of edging meet and hang off one corner of the pillow as shown. Stuff the pillow. If you're using a commercial pillow form, you might want to take out some of the stuffing so the felted pillow is flatter.

ACKNOWLEDGMENTS

I'd like to thank feltmakers throughout the ages: bootmakers in Scandinavia; rugs makers in Iran; hat makers in Turkey; and the ancient hordes who changed the world, riding in from the East on felted saddles. I'm proud to be part of the tradition of the oldest textile process in the world. I thank everyone who has ever squeezed raw fleece in their hands and instantly had a head full of possibilities.

Individual thanks go to Mary E. Burkett, OBE who truly is the grande dame of the modern felt movement, and to the staff and members of the International Feltmakers Association in England. Pat Spark deserves a big "thank you" for her impressive work in organizing the North American Feltmakers Network in newsletter and website form.

Feltmaking is international, and I have been inspired by a wealth of friendships: Lene Neilsen and Annette Damgaard in Denmark; Jori Johnston of Japan; Kristin Jonsdottir and Anna Dora Karlsdottir of Iceland; May Jacobsen Hvistendahl of Norway; Gunilla Paetau Sjoberg of Sweden; Katherina Thomas of Germany; Lyda Vermeulen-Rump and Joke van Zinderen of Holland; Leena Sipila of Finland; Meike Dalal-Laurenson, Jeanette Appleton, Sarah Lawrence, Sheila Smith, and Maggie Whiteman among many in England; and my fellow American felters who inspired me, Karen Page, Layne Goldsmith, Beth Beede, and Joan Livingstone. Together with so many others, we share, teach, and continue the feltmaking traditions.

A big "thank you" to my amazing editor Marthe Le Van for her patience and intelligence; my good pal, Jane Voorhees, for her encouragement; and to Melissa Etheridge for providing the music and words that kept me working.

Chad Alice Hagen. *Kan Ma Kan - Recut* (detail), *1993*. 80½ x 57 inches (204.4 x 144.8 cm), Hand-felted wool. Photo by Gerald Sedgewick.

Chad Alice Hagen. Hand felted hats. Merino wool, dye. Photo by Tim Barnwell.

ABOUT THE AUTHOR

Chad Alice Hagen's years of exploration with hand-felted wool led her to her passion: surface resist dyeing. They've also yielded an impressive body of work and highly developed skills—both of which she shares with people around the world.

Chad received her B.A. in Art and M.S. in Textile Design from the University of Wisconsin-Madison. She also has an M.F.A. from the Cranbrook Academy of Art.

Chad has taught feltmaking to adults and children in the United States since 1984 and in Europe since 2000.

Her work has been featured on the covers of FIBERARTS Magazine, Surface Design Journal, and Shuttle, Spindle & Dyepot. It has been the subject of articles and photographs in publications including *American Craft Magazine*, *Echoes*, and several *FIBERARTS* design books.

Chad has written articles on the textile arts for *FIBERARTS*, *Echoes*, *Surface Design Journal*, and *Shuttle, Spindle & Dyepot*.

Her hand-felted wool has been exhibited throughout the United States and in Mexico, Japan, India, England, and Denmark. Chad's artwork is included in the collections of the Mint Museum of Art & Design in Charlotte, NC; The Minneapolis Institute of Art; The University of Wisconsin-Madison; the corporate collections of B.F. Goodrich and Westinghouse; and many private collections.

TEMPLATES

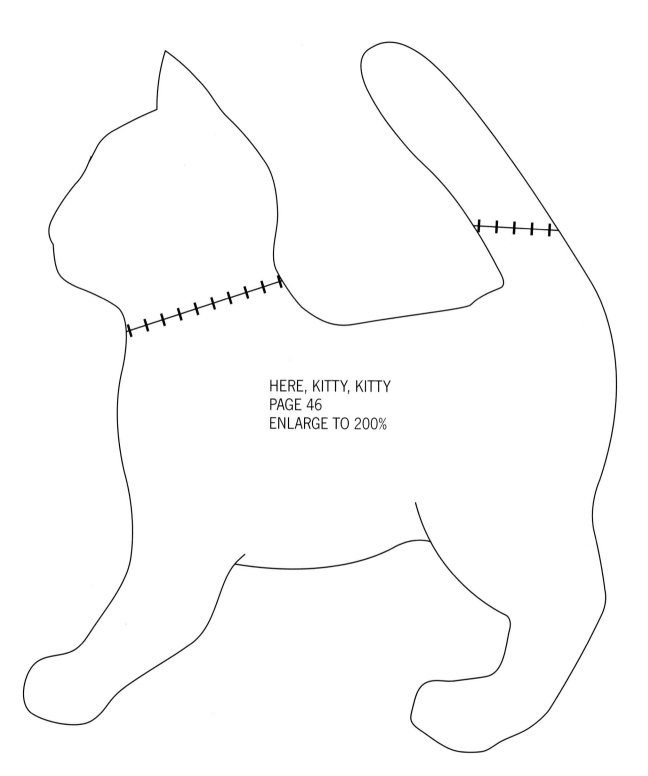

HERE, KITTY, KITTY
PAGE 46
ENLARGE TO 200%

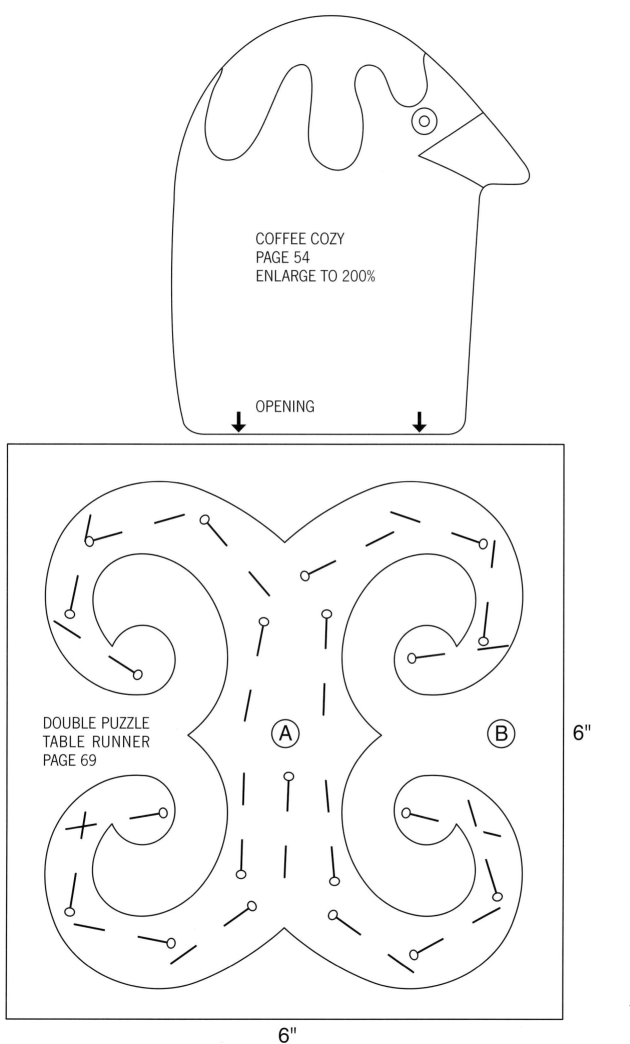

COFFEE COZY
PAGE 54
ENLARGE TO 200%

OPENING

DOUBLE PUZZLE
TABLE RUNNER
PAGE 69

(A)

(B)

6"

6"

INDEX

Agitation, 18
Batt, 9
Basic feltmaking kit, 17
Cortex cells, 10
Crimp, 10
Dreadlocks, 21
Felt, 8
Flat felt, 22
Fulling, 25
Merino wool, 11
pH, 12
Pelssau/Gotland wool, 11
Pinch test, 25
Prefelt, 26
Resist felt, 27
Root, 21
Rinsing, 15
Safety, 17
Scales, 9
Shingle, 22
Sliver, 9
Soap, 12
Soap gel, 13
Soap gel mix, 14
Soap containers, 14
Solid felt balls, 18
Solid felt snakes, 20
Thickness of fiber, 10
Vinegar rinse, 15
Water, 15
Wetting mix, 14
Wool, 9